CREDITS

DESIGNS — Kim Hargreaves

PHOTOGRAPHY — Graham Watts

STYLING — Kim Hargreaves

HAIR & MAKE-UP — Diana Fisher

MODELS — Kristie Stubley & Lee Davies

EDITOR — Kathleen Hargreaves

EDITORIAL DESIGN — Graham Watts

LAYOUTS — Angela Lin

PATTERNS — Sue Whiting & Trisha McKenzie

Copyright Kim Hargreaves 2009
First published in 2009 by Kim Hargreaves
Intake Cottage, 26 Underbank Old Road, Holmfirth
West Yorkshire, HD9 1EA, England

British Library Cataloguing in Publication Data
A catalogue record for this book is available from the British Library

ISBN-10   1—906487—05—8
ISBN-13   978—1—906487—05—8

4

CONTENTS

THE DESIGNS 7

THE PATTERNS 56

INFORMATION 102

INDEX 105

THE
DESIGNS

As the light of summer fades and autumn approaches, its vibrant shades are replaced with honest tender tones. Shapes are cosy soft and sensual, inviting a new gentle elegance. Effortless and unassuming, these classic pieces present the perfect backdrop for this tale of true romance...

Kristie is wearing
RONNIE *textured*
Sloppy Joe with
cabled trims

BILLIE a cosy
hooded wrap
cardigan.

SID a chic sweater
worked in mohair,
with deep raglans.

12

THEA a double
fronted jacket
featuring a
notched collar.

15

Kristie wears
THEA a double
fronted jacket,
worn with KAT
cabled hat.

MAGGIE a neat
fitting cardigan
with garter stitch
curved peplum.

18

Kristie is wearing
AURA lacy wrap
& opposite
LAUREN an
elegant blousy
cardigan, close
fitting at the waist.

20

This page JEN
a cute cropped
cardigan, opposite
NAT an A-line
cabled jacket.

22

Opposite Kristie is
wearing JEN a
cropped cardigan,
& this page THEA
short sleeved jacket,
Lee wears ARCHIE
raglan sweater.

*Lee wears
ARCHIE sweater
with garter stitch
raglan yoke.*

BEA a pretty
cardigan worn
with AURA,
lacy scarf.

29

This page MAGGIE
a fitted cardigan,
opposite CHRISTY
double fronted cardigan
with shawl neck.

34

To Knit

AAREN a cabled
mini dress worn
with KAT textured
& cabled hat.

37

Kristie is wearing
LUCKY a textured
beret with contrasting
coloured pom pom,
Lee wears ED classic
cabled sweater.

38

Kristie wears
FAY sweater with
eyelet & button
details, Lee wears
ED a classic
cabled sweater.

This page FAY
a scooped necked
sweater, opposite
VIVIENNE graceful
sweater with button
trim on a garter
stitch yoke

42

LUCKY a cute
textured beret with
contrast coloured
pom pom.

47

Kristie is wearing
EFFIE a striking
button through
sweater with
frill details.

EDIE a classic
sweater featuring
deep raglans
& wide neckline.

Kristie wears,
KAT a cabled hat
& opposite, AURA
a luscious lacy wrap.

THE
PATTERNS

VIVIENNE
FITTED SWEATER WITH GARTER STITCH YOKE

Recommendation
Suitable for the knitter with a little experience
Please see pages 43-45 for photographs.

	XS	S	M	L	XL	XXL	
To fit	**81**	**86**	**91**	**97**	**102**	**109**	cm
bust	32	34	36	38	40	43	in

Rowan Pure Cashmere DK
	10	11	11	12	12	13 x 25gm
Photographed in Greige

Needles
1 pair 3mm (no 11) (US 2/3) needles
1 pair 3¼mm (no 10) (US 3) needles
3mm (no 11) (US 2/3) circular needle

Buttons – 12 (12: 12: 12: 13: 13)

Tension
27 sts and 37 rows to 10 cm measured
over stocking stitch, 27 sts and 44 rows
to 10 cm measured over garter stitch,
both using 3¼mm (US 3) needles.

BACK
Cast on 107 (113: 119: 127: 133: 145) sts
using 3mm (US 2/3) needles.
Work in garter st for 3 rows, ending with a
RS row.
Row 4 (WS): K1, *P1, K1, rep from * to end.
Row 5: As row 4.
Last 2 rows form moss st.
Work in moss st for a further 9 rows, ending
with a WS row.
Change to 3¼mm (US 3) needles.
Beg with a K row, work in st st for 2 (2: 4: 4: 4:
4) rows, ending with a WS row.
Next row (dec) (RS): K2, K2tog, K to last 4 sts,
K2tog tbl, K2.
105 (111: 117: 125: 131: 143) sts.
Working decreases as set by last row, dec 1 st
at each end of 8th and 4 foll 8th rows.
95 (101: 107: 115: 121: 133) sts.
Work 13 rows, ending with a WS row.
Next row (inc) (RS): K3, M1, K to last 3 sts,
M1, K3. 97 (103: 109: 117: 123: 135) sts.
Working all increases as set by last row, inc
1 st at each end of 10th and 6 foll 10th rows.
111 (117: 123: 131: 137: 149) sts.
Work 7 (7: 9: 9: 9: 9) rows, ending with a
WS row.
Shape raglan armholes
Now working in garter st throughout, cont as
folls:
Cast off 8 sts at beg of next 2 rows.
95 (101: 107: 115: 121: 133) sts.**
Work 2 rows.
Next row (dec) (RS): K3, K2tog, K to last 5 sts,
K2tog tbl, K3.
93 (99: 105: 113: 119: 131) sts.
Working all raglan armhole decreases as set by
last row, dec 1 st at each end of 4th and 7 (8:
6: 5: 6: 4) foll 4th rows, then on foll 0 (0: 5: 7:
7: 14) alt rows. 77 (81: 81: 87: 91: 93) sts.
Work 3 (3: 1: 1: 1: 1) rows, ending with a
WS row.
Shape back neck
Next row (RS): K3, K2tog, K7 (8: 8: 12: 12:
12) and turn, leaving rem sts on a holder.
Work each side of neck separately.

Dec 1 st at neck edge of next 5 (5: 5: 6: 6: 6)
rows, then on foll 0 (0: 0: 1: 1: 1) alt row **and
at same time** dec 1 st at raglan armhole edge
of 4th (2nd: 2nd: 2nd: 2nd: 2nd) and foll 0 (1:
1: 3: 3: 3) alt rows. 5 sts.
Work 0 (0: 0: 1: 1: 1) row, ending with a
WS row.
Next row (RS): K2, sl 1, K2tog, psso.
Next row: K3.
Next row: sl 1, K2tog, psso.
Next row: K1 and fasten off.
With RS facing, rejoin yarn to rem sts, cast off
centre 53 (55: 55: 53: 57: 59) sts, K to last 5
sts, K2tog tbl, K3.
Complete to match first side, reversing
shapings.

FRONT
Work as given for back to **.
Divide for front opening
Next row (RS): K44 (47: 50: 54: 57: 63)
and slip these sts onto a holder, K to end.
51 (54: 57: 61: 64: 70) sts.
Work each side of neck separately.
Work 1 row.
XS and XL sizes only
Next row (RS): K2, K2tog, yfwd (to make first
buttonhole), K3, yfwd, K2tog tbl (to make
eyelet), K to last 5 sts, K2tog tbl, K3. 50 (-: -: -:
63: -) sts.
Making a further 4 (-: -: -: 5: -) buttonholes
as set by last row on every foll 8th row and
noting that no further reference will be made
to buttonholes, cont as folls:
Next row: Knit.
These 2 rows set the sts – 7 st front band
marked by vertical line of eyelets and raglan
armhole decreases worked as given for back.
S, M, L and XXL sizes only
Next row (RS): K7, yfwd, K2tog tbl (to make
eyelet), K to last 5 sts, K2tog tbl, K3. - (53: 56:
60: -: 69) sts.
Next row: Knit.
These 2 rows set the sts – 7 st front band
marked by vertical line of eyelets and raglan
armhole decreases worked as given for back.

Work – (2: 2: 2: -: 4) rows, dec – (0: 0: 0: -: 1) st at raglan armhole edge on 3rd row and ending with a WS row. - (53: 56: 60: -: 68) sts.

Next row (RS): K2, K2tog, yfwd (to make first buttonhole), K3, yfwd, K2tog tbl (to make eyelet), K to last - (5: 5: 5: -: 0) sts, (K2tog tbl, K3) - (1: 1: 1: -: 0) times. - (52: 55: 59: -: 68) sts.

Making a further - (4: 4: 4: -: 5) buttonholes as set by last row on every foll 8th row and noting that no further reference will be made to buttonholes, cont as folls:

Next row: Knit.

All sizes

Keeping sts correct as set, dec 1 st at raglan armhole edge on 3rd (3rd: 3rd: 3rd: 3rd: next) and 7 (7: 5: 4: 6: 3) foll 4th rows, then on foll 0 (0: 5: 7: 7: 14) alt rows.

42 (44: 44: 47: 49: 50) sts.

Work 3 (3: 1: 1: 1: 1) rows, ending with a WS row.

Shape neck

Next row (RS): Patt 30 (31: 31: 30: 32: 33) sts and slip these sts onto a holder, K to last 5 sts, K2tog tbl, K3.

11 (12: 12: 16: 16: 16) sts.

Dec 1 st at neck edge of next 5 (5: 5: 6: 6: 6) rows, then on foll 0 (0: 0: 1: 1: 1) alt row **and at same time** dec 1 st at raglan armhole edge of 4th (2nd: 2nd: 2nd: 2nd: 2nd) and foll 0 (1: 1: 3: 3: 3) alt rows. 5 sts.

Work 0 (0: 0: 1: 1: 1) row, ending with a WS row.

Next row (RS): sl 1, K2tog, psso, K2.

Next row: K3.

Next row: sl 1, K2tog, psso.

Next row: K1 and fasten off.

With **WS** facing, rejoin yarn to rem sts, cast on 7 sts, K to end. 51 (54: 57: 61: 64: 70) sts.

Next row (RS): K3, K2tog, K to last 9 sts, K2tog, yfwd (to make eyelet), K7.

50 (53: 56: 60: 63: 69) sts.

Next row: Knit.

These 2 rows set the sts – 7 st front band marked by vertical line of eyelets and raglan armhole decreases worked as given for back. Complete to match first side, reversing shapings, omitting buttonholes and working first row of neck shaping as folls:

Next row (RS): K3, K2tog, K7 (8: 8: 12: 12: 12) and turn, leaving rem 30 (31: 31: 30: 32: 33) sts on a holder.

11 (12: 12: 16: 16: 16) sts.

LEFT SLEEVE

First section

Cast on 35 (36: 36: 37: 39: 40) sts using 3mm (US 2/3) needles.

Work in garter st for 2 rows, ending with a WS row.

Row 3 (RS): K5, yfwd, K2tog, K to end.

Row 4: P0 (1: 1: 0: 0: 1), *K1, P1, rep from * to last 5 sts, K5.

Row 5: K5, yfwd, K2tog, *P1, K1, rep from * to last 0 (1: 1: 0: 0: 1) st, P0 (1: 1: 0: 0: 1).

Last 2 rows set the sts.

Cont as set for a further 23 rows, inc 1 st at end of 12th of these rows and ending with a WS row.

36 (37: 37: 38: 40: 41) sts.

Break yarn and leave sts on a holder.

Second section

Cast on 24 (25: 25: 26: 28: 29) sts using 3mm (US 2/3) needles.

Work in garter st for 3 rows, ending with a **RS** row.

Row 4 (WS): K0 (1: 1: 0: 0: 1), *P1, K1, rep from * to end.

Row 5: *K1, P1, rep from * to last 0 (1: 1: 0: 0: 1) st, K0 (1: 1: 0: 0: 1).

Last 2 rows form moss st.

Work in moss st for a further 23 rows, inc 1 st at beg of 12th of these rows and ending with a WS row.

25 (26: 26: 27: 29: 30) sts.

Join sections

Change to 3¼mm (US 3) needles.

Row 29 (RS): K2, M1, K to last 7 sts of second section, now holding WS of first section against RS of second section K tog first st of first section with next st of second section, (K tog next st of first section with next st of second section) 6 times, K to last 2 sts of first section, M1, K2. 56 (58: 58: 60: 64: 66) sts.

***Beg with a P row and working all increases as set by last row, cont in st st, shaping sides by inc 1 st at each end of 10th and 2 (0: 6: 10: 3: 1) foll 10th rows, then on every foll 12th row until there are 78 (80: 82: 86: 88: 90) sts. Cont straight until sleeve measures 45 (46: 46: 47: 48: 49) cm, ending with a WS row.

Shape raglan

Now working in garter st throughout, cont as folls:

Cast off 8 sts at beg of next 2 rows.

62 (64: 66: 70: 72: 74) sts.

Work 4 rows.

Working all raglan decreases in same way as back raglan armhole decreases, dec 1 st at each end of next and 4 (4: 4: 2: 4: 5) foll 6th rows, then on 4 (5: 5: 9: 7: 7) foll 4th rows.

44 (44: 46: 46: 48: 48) sts.

Work 3 rows, ending with a WS row.

Cast off.

RIGHT SLEEVE

First section

Cast on 24 (25: 25: 26: 28: 29) sts using 3mm (US 2/3) needles.

Work in garter st for 3 rows, ending with a **RS** row.

Row 4 (WS): *K1, P1, rep from * to last 0 (1: 1: 0: 0: 1) st, K0 (1: 1: 0: 0: 1).

Row 5: K0 (1: 1: 0: 0: 1), *P1, K1, rep from * to end.

Last 2 rows form moss st.

Work in moss st for a further 23 rows, inc 1 st at end of 12th of these rows and ending with a WS row. 25 (26: 26: 27: 29: 30) sts.

Break yarn and leave sts on a holder.

Second section

Cast on 35 (36: 36: 37: 39: 40) sts using 3mm (US 2/3) needles.

Work in garter st for 2 rows, ending with a WS row.

Row 3 (RS): K to last 7 sts, K2tog, yfwd, K5.

Row 4: K5, *P1, K1, rep from * to last 0 (1: 1: 0: 0: 1) st, P0 (1: 1: 0: 0: 1)

Row 5: P0 (1: 1: 0: 0: 1), *K1, P1, rep from * to last 7 sts, K2tog, yfwd, K5.

Last 2 rows set the sts.

Cont as set for a further 23 rows, inc 1 st at beg of 12th of these rows and ending with a WS row. 36 (37: 37: 38: 40: 41) sts.

Join sections

Change to 3¼mm (US 3) needles.

Row 29 (RS): K2, M1, K to last 7 sts of second section, now holding RS of first section against WS of second section K tog next st of second section with first st of first section, (K tog next st of second section with next st of first section) 6 times, K to last 2 sts of first section, M1, K2. 56 (58: 58: 60: 64: 66) sts.

Complete as given for left sleeve from ***.

MAKING UP

Press all pieces using a warm iron over a damp cloth.

Join all 4 raglan seams using back stitch or mattress stitch if preferred.

Neckband

With RS facing and using 3mm (US 2/3) circular needle, slip 30 (31: 31: 30: 32: 33) sts from right front holder onto right needle, rejoin yarn and pick up and knit 9 (9: 9: 13: 13: 13) sts up right side of front neck, place marker on right needle, pick up and knit 42 (42: 44: 44: 46: 46) sts from top of right sleeve placing marker between centre 2 sts, place marker on right needle, pick up and knit 9 (9: 9: 13: 13: 13) sts down right side of back neck, 53 (55: 55: 53: 57: 59) sts from back, and 9 (9: 9: 13: 13: 13) sts up left side of back neck, place marker on right needle, pick up and knit 42 (42: 44: 44: 46: 46) sts from top of left sleeve placing marker between centre 2 sts, place marker on right needle, pick up and knit 9 (9: 9: 13: 13: 13) sts down left side of front neck, then patt 30 (31: 31: 30: 32: 33) sts from left front holder.

233 (237: 241: 253: 265: 269) sts, 6 markers in total.

Row 1 and every foll alt row (WS): Knit.

Row 2: K7, yfwd, K2tog tbl (to make eyelet), *K to within 4 sts of marker, K2tog tbl, K4 (marker is between centre 2 sts of these 4 sts), K2tog, rep from * 5 times more, K to last 9 sts, K2tog, yfwd (to make eyelet), K7.

221 (225: 229: 241: 253: 257) sts.

Row 4 (buttonhole row): K2, K2tog, yfwd (to make last buttonhole), K3, yfwd, K2tog tbl (to make eyelet), K to last 9 sts, K2tog, yfwd (to make eyelet), K7.

Row 6: As row 2.

209 (213: 217: 229: 241: 245) sts.

Row 8: K7, yfwd, K2tog tbl (to make eyelet), K to last 9 sts, K2tog, yfwd (to make eyelet), K7.

Row 10: As row 2.

Cast off rem 197 (201: 205: 217: 229: 233) sts knitwise (on **WS**).

Join side and sleeve seams. Sew on buttons, attaching 3 buttons to each cuff opening as in photograph.

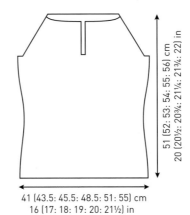

41 (43.5: 45.5: 48.5: 51: 55) cm
16 (17: 18: 19: 20: 21½) in

51 (52: 53: 54: 55: 56) cm
20 (20½: 20¾: 21¼: 21¾: 22) in

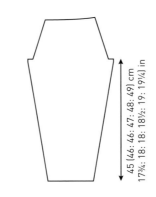

45 (46: 46: 47: 48: 49) cm
17¾: 18: 18: 18½: 19: 19¼) in

THEA

DOUBLE FRONTED JACKET WITH LONG OR SHORT SLEEVES

Recommendation
Suitable for the knitter with a little experience.
Please see pages 15, 16, & 25 for photographs.

	XS	S	M	L	XL	XXL	
To fit	**81**	**86**	**91**	**97**	**102**	**109**	cm
	32	34	36	38	40	43	in

Rowan Kid Classic
Long sleeved version

	7	8	8	9	9	10 x 50gm

Short sleeved version

	6	7	7	7	8	9 x 50gm

Photographed in Smoke & Bittersweet

Needles
1 pair 4 mm (no 8) (US 6) needles – for short
sleeve version only
1 pair 4 ½ mm (no 7) (US 7) needles

Buttons – 6 for long sleeve version
– 8 for short sleeve version

Tension
21 sts and 27 rows to 10 cm measured over
stocking stitch using 4 ½ mm (US 7) needles.

Special abbreviations
Right dec = Sl 1, K1, psso, sl st now on right
needle back onto left needle, lift 2nd st on
left needle over this st and off needle, and
then slip rem st back onto right needle - 2 sts
decreased.
Left dec = Sl 1, K2tog, psso - 2 sts decreased.

BACK
Cast on 92 (96: 100: 106: 112: 120) sts, using
4 ½ mm (US 7) needles.
Row 1 (RS): K1 (0: 1: 0: 0: 0), P2 (1: 2: 2: 1:
1), *K2, P2; rep from * to last 1 (3: 1: 0: 3: 3)
sts, K1 (2: 1: 0: 2: 2), P0 (1: 0: 0: 1: 1).
Row 2: P1 (0: 1: 0: 0: 0), K2 (1: 2: 2: 1: 1),
*P2, K2; rep from * to last 1 (3: 1: 0: 3: 3) sts,
P1 (2: 1: 0: 2: 2), K0 (1: 0: 0: 1: 1).
These 2 rows form the rib patt.
Work a further 16 rows, ending with a WS row.
Beg with a K row cont in st st as folls:
Work 2 rows.
Start side and dart shaping
Place a marker around the 23rd (24th: 25th:
26th: 27th: 28th) sts in from each end of last
row, this marker indicates the position of the dart.
Next row (RS)(dec): K2, K2tog, K to 1 st
before first marked st, right dec, K to 1 st
before second marked st, left dec, K to last
4 sts, K2tog tbl, K2.
86 (90: 94: 100: 106: 114) sts.
Work 7 (7: 9: 9: 9: 9) rows, ending with a
WS row.
Dec as before on next row and foll 6th (8th: 8th:
10th: 10th: 10th) row, ending with a **RS** row.
74 (78: 82: 88: 94: 102) sts.
Work 19 rows straight ending with a WS row.
Next row (RS)(inc): K2, M1, K to first marked
stitch, M1, K1, M1, K to second marked st, M1,
K1, M1, K to last 2 sts, M1, K2.
80 (84: 88: 94: 100: 108) sts.
Work 11 rows, ending with a WS row.
Inc as before on next row and foll 12th row.
92 (96: 100: 106: 112: 120) sts.
Remove markers.
Work 11 (11: 11: 9: 9: 9) rows.
Work should measure approx 34 (34: 35:
35: 35: 35) cm, ending with a WS row.
Shape armholes
Cast off 4 sts at beg of next 2 rows.
84 (88: 92: 98: 104: 112) sts.
Dec 1 st at each end of next 5 (5: 7: 7: 9: 11)
rows, and then on 5 (5: 4: 5: 4: 4) foll alt rows,
and then on foll 4th row.
62 (66: 68: 72: 76: 80) sts.

Work straight until armhole measures 18 (19:
19: 20: 21: 22) cm, ending with a WS row.
Shape shoulders and back neck
Cast off 6 (6: 7: 7: 7: 8) sts at beg of next
2 rows.
Cast off 6 (6: 6: 7: 7: 8) sts, K until 9 (10:
10: 10: 11: 11) sts on right needle and turn,
leaving rem sts on a holder.
Work each side of neck separately.
Cast off 4 sts at beg of next row.
Cast off rem 5 (6: 6: 6: 7: 7) sts.
With RS facing, rejoin yarn to sts from holder,
cast off centre 20 (22: 22: 24: 26: 26) sts,
K to end.
Complete to match first side, reversing
shapings.

LEFT FRONT
Cast on 56 (58: 61: 64: 68: 72) sts using
4 ½ mm (US 7) needles.
Row 1 (RS): K1 (0: 1: 0: 0: 0), P2 (1: 2: 2: 1:
1), *K2, P2; rep from * to last 21 (21: 22: 22:
23: 23) sts, (P1, K1) to last 1 (1: 0: 0: 1: 1) st,
P1 (1: 0: 0: 1: 1).
Row 2: K1 (1: 0: 0: 1: 1), (P1, K1) 10 (10: 11:
11: 11: 11) times, (K2, P2) to last 3 (1: 3: 2: 1:
1) sts, K2 (1: 2: 2: 1: 1), P1 (0: 1: 0: 0: 0).
Row 3: K1 (0: 1: 0: 0: 0), P2 (1: 2: 2: 1: 1),
*K2, P2; rep from * to last 21 (21: 22: 22: 23:
23) sts, (K1, P1) to last 1 (1: 0: 0: 1: 1) st, K1
(1: 0: 0: 1: 1).
Row 4: P1 (1: 0: 0: 1: 1), (K1, P1) 10 (10: 11:
11: 11: 11) times, (K2, P2) to last 3 (1: 3: 2:
1: 1) sts, K2 (1: 2: 2: 1: 1), P1 (0: 1: 0: 0: 0).
These 4 rows set the stitches, 21 (21: 22:
22: 23: 23) sts worked in double moss st for
the front band and rem stitches in rib as given
for back.
Work a further 14 rows, ending with a WS row.
Next row (RS): K to last 21 (21: 22: 22: 23:
23) sts, patt to end.
Next row: Patt 21 (21: 22: 22: 23: 23) sts,
P to end.
Place a marker around the 23rd (24th:
25th: 26th: 27th: 28th) st in from end
of last row.

59

Start side and dart shaping

Next row (RS)(dec): K2, K2tog, K to 1 st before marked st, right dec, K to last 21 (21: 22: 22: 23: 23) sts, patt to end.

53 (55: 58: 61: 65: 69) sts.

Work 7 (7: 9: 9: 9: 9) rows, ending with a WS row.

Dec as before on next row and foll 6th (8th: 8th: 10th: 10th: 10th) row, ending with a **RS** row.

47 (49: 52: 55: 59: 63) sts.

Work 19 rows straight ending with a WS row.

Shape front slope and lower collar

Row 1 (RS)(inc): K2, M1, K to marked stitch, M1, K1, M1, K to last 25 (25: 26: 26: 27: 27) sts, K2tog, K2, M1, patt to end.

50 (52: 55: 58: 62: 66) sts.

Work 5 rows.

Row 7 (RS)(inc): K to last 22 (22: 23: 23: 24: 24) sts, M1, patt to end.

51 (53: 56: 59: 63: 67) sts.

Work 5 rows.

Row 13 (RS)(inc): K2, M1, K to marked stitch, M1, K1, M1, K to last 23 (23: 24: 24: 25: 25) sts, M1, patt to end.

55 (57: 60: 63: 67: 71) sts.

Work 5 rows.

Row 19 (RS)(inc): K to last 24 (24: 25: 25: 26: 26) sts, M1, patt to end.

56 (58: 61: 64: 68: 72) sts

Work 5 rows.

Row 25 (RS)(inc): K2, M1, K to marked stitch, M1, K1, M1, K to last 29 (29: 30: 30: 31: 31) sts, K2tog, K2, M1, patt to end.

59 (61: 64: 67: 71: 75) sts.

This completes the side and dart shaping.

Cont shaping front edge and collar as folls:

Work 5 rows, ending with a WS row.

Row 31: Knit to last 26 (26: 27: 27: 28: 28) sts, M1, patt to end.

60 (62: 65: 68: 72: 76) sts.

Work 5 (5: 5: 3: 3: 3) rows.

Cont shaping lower collar by inc 1 st as before on every 6th row until 30 (30: 31: 31: 33: 33) are worked in double moss st, and shaping front slope by dec 1 st as before on 1 (2: 2: 3: 4: 4) foll 28th (20th: 20th:16th: 12th: 12th) rows (counted from last dec), and **at the same time** shape armhole as folls:

Shape armhole

Keeping front slope and lower collar shaping correct, cast off 4 sts at beg of next row.

Work 1 row.

Dec 1 st at armhole edge of next 5 (5: 7: 7: 9: 11) rows, then on 5 (5: 4: 5: 4: 4) foll alt rows, and then on foll 4th row.

Keeping front slope and collar shaping correct, cont on stitches as set until left front is 21 (25: 25: 25: 25: 25) rows shorter than back to beg of shoulder shaping, ending with a **RS** row.

Shape collar

Cast off 30 (30: 31: 31: 33: 33) sts, P to end.

Cont dec at front slope, where applicable, until 17 (18: 19: 20: 21: 23) sts rem.

Work straight until left front matches back to beg of shoulder shaping, ending with a WS row.

Shape shoulder

Cast off 6 (6: 7: 7: 7: 8) sts at beg of next row and 6 (6: 6: 7: 7: 8) sts at beg of foll alt row.

Work 1 row.

Cast off rem 5 (6: 6: 6: 7: 7) sts.

RIGHT FRONT

Cast on 56 (58: 61: 64: 68: 72) sts using 4 ½ mm (US 7) needles.

Row 1 (RS): P1 (1: 0: 0: 1: 1), (K1, P1) 10 (10: 11: 11: 11: 11) times, *P2, K2; rep from * to last 3 (1: 3: 2: 1: 1) sts, P2 (1: 2: 2: 1: 1), K1 (0: 1: 0: 0: 0).

Row 2: P1 (0: 1: 0: 0: 0), K2 (1: 2: 2: 1: 1), (P2, K2) to last 21 (21: 22: 22: 23: 23) sts, (K1, P1) to last 1 (1: 0: 0: 1: 1) st, K1 (0: 1: 0: 0: 1).

Row 3 (RS): K1 (1: 0: 0: 1: 1), (P1, K1) 10 (10: 11: 11: 11: 11) times, *P2, K2; rep from * to last 3 (1: 3: 2: 1: 1) sts, P2 (1: 2: 2: 1: 1), K1 (0: 1: 0: 0: 0).

Row 4: P1 (0: 1: 0: 0: 0), K2 (1: 2: 2: 1: 1), (P2, K2) to last 21 (21: 22: 22: 23: 23) sts, (P1, K1) to last 1 (1: 0: 0: 1: 1) st, P1 (1: 0: 0: 1: 1).

These 4 rows set the stitches, 21 (21: 22: 22: 23: 23) sts worked in double moss st for the front band and rem stitches in rib as given for back.

Work a further 14 rows, ending with a WS row.

Next row (RS): Patt 21 (21: 22: 22: 23: 23) sts, K to end.

Next row: P to last 21 (21: 22: 22: 23: 23) sts, patt to end.

Place a marker around the 23rd (24th: 25th: 26th: 27th: 28th) st in from beg of last row.

Start side and dart shaping

Next row (RS)(dec): Patt 21 (21: 22: 22: 23: 23) sts, K to 1 st before marked st, left dec, K to last 4 sts, K2tog tbl, K2.

53 (55: 58: 61: 65: 69) sts.

Work 1 (1: 3: 5: 5: 5) rows.

Next row (RS)(buttonhole row): Patt 4 sts, *patt 2tog tbl, (yon) twice, patt 2 tog *, patt 5 (5: 6: 6: 7: 7), rep from * to *, work to end.

Work 5 (5: 7: 7: 7: 7) rows, ending with a WS row.

Dec as before on next row.

50 (52: 55: 58: 62: 66) sts.

Work 5 (7: 5: 5: 5: 5) rows ending with a WS row.

Next row (RS)(dec)(buttonhole row): Patt 4 sts, *patt 2tog tbl, (yon) twice, patt 2 tog *, patt 5 (5: 6: 6: 7: 7), rep from * to *, work to 1 st before marked st, left dec, K to last 4 sts, K2tog, tbl, K2.

47 (49: 52: 55: 59: 63) sts.

Work 13 rows ending with a WS row.

Next row (RS)(buttonhole row): Patt 4 sts, *patt 2tog tbl, (yon) twice, patt 2 tog *, patt 5 (5: 6: 6: 7: 7), rep from * to *, work to end.

Work 5 rows, ending with a WS row.

Shape front slope and collar

Row 1 (RS)(inc): Patt 21 (21: 22: 22: 23: 23) sts, M1, K2, K2tog tbl, K to marked stitch, M1, K1, M1, K to last 2 sts, M1, K2.

50 (52: 55: 58: 62: 66) sts.

Complete as given for left front reversing all shapings.

LONG SLEEVES (work both the same)

Cast on 61 (63: 63: 67: 67: 71) sts using 4 ½ mm (US 7) needles.

Row 1 (RS): K1, (P1, K1) to end.

Row 2: P1, (K1, P1) to end.

Row 3: Work as row 2.

Row 4: Work as row 1.

These 4 rows form the double moss st pattern.

Keeping patt correct dec 1 st at each end of next row, then on 2 foll 4th rows, and then on 1 foll 6th row.

53 (55: 55: 59: 59: 63) sts.

Work 3 rows ending with a WS row.

Beg with a K row cont in st st as folls:

Work 2 (2: 2: 4: 4: 4) rows.

Next row (RS) (dec): K2, K2tog, K to last 4 sts, K2tog tbl, K2.

51 (53: 53: 57: 57: 61) sts.

Work 3 (5: 5: 5: 5: 7) rows.

Dec as before on next row.

49 (51: 51: 55: 55: 59) sts

Work straight for 17 rows, ending with a WS row.

Next row (RS)(inc): K2, M1, K to last 2 sts, M1, K2.

Work 9 rows.

Inc as before on next row and 5 (5: 5: 3: 3: 2) foll 10th rows and then **for L, XL & XXL** sizes only, every foll 12th row to 69 (69: 73) sts.

63 (65: 65: 69: 69: 73) sts.

Work straight until sleeve measures 44 (45: 46: 47: 48: 49) cm from cast on edge, ending with a WS row.

Shape top

Cast off 4 sts at beg of next 2 rows.

55 (57: 57: 61: 61: 65) sts.

Dec 1 st at each end of next 3 rows, then on foll alt row, and then on every foll 4th row to 39 (41: 41: 43: 43: 47) sts.

Work 1 row ending with a WS row.

Dec 1 st at each end of next row and every foll alt to 31 (31: 31: 37: 37: 39) sts and then on every row until 21 (21: 21: 23: 23: 25) sts rem.

Cast off.

SHORT SLEEVES
Left sleeve
Cuff front

Cast on 37 (39: 39: 41: 41: 43) sts using 4 ½ mm (US 7) needles and work 18 (20: 20: 20: 22: 22) rows in double moss st, setting stitches as given for lower edge of long sleeve.

Break yarn and leave stitches on a spare needle.

Cuff back

Cast on 27 (27: 27: 29: 29: 31) sts using 4 ½ mm (US 7) needles and work 18 (20: 20: 20: 22: 22) rows in double moss st as for cuff front.

Join pieces together

Work in patt to last 7 sts of cuff back, now with needles parallel and cuff back at the **front**, taking 1 st from each needle together as one, patt 7 sts, patt to end.

57 (59: 59: 63: 63: 67) sts.

Work 3 more rows in pattern.

Cast off.

Upper sleeve

With cast-off edge of cuff uppermost, **cuff back** to the right and using 4mm (US 6) needles, pick up and knit 57 (59: 59: 63: 63: 67) sts evenly across the cast off edge and turn, purl one row.

Beg with a K row, work 6 rows in st st.

Change to 4 ½ mm (US 7) needles and cont in st st shaping sides as folls:

Next row (RS)(inc): K2, M1, K to last 2 sts, M1, K2.

59 (61: 61: 65: 65: 69) sts.

Work 7 rows.

Inc as before on next row and foll 8th row.

63 (65: 65: 69: 69: 73) sts.

Work straight until sleeve measures 12 (13: 13: 14: 14: 15) cm from beg of st st, ending with a WS row.

Shape top

Shape top as given for long sleeve.

Right sleeve
Cuff back

Cast on 27 (27: 27: 29: 29: 31) sts using 4 ½ mm (US 7) needles and work 18 (20: 20: 20: 22: 22) rows in double moss st as for left cuff front.

Break yarn and leave stitches on a spare needle.

Cuff front

Cast on 37 (39: 39: 41: 41: 43) sts using 4 ½ mm (US 7) needles and work 18 (20: 20: 20: 22: 22) rows in double moss st as for cuff back.

Join pieces together

Work in patt to last 7 sts of cuff front, now with needles parallel and cuff back at the **front**, taking 1 st from each needle together as one, patt 7 sts, patt to end.

57 (59: 59: 63: 63: 67) sts.

Complete as given for left sleeve.

MAKING UP

Press all pieces using a warm iron over a damp cloth.

Join both shoulder seams using backstitch or mattress st if preferred.

Collar

Cast on 83 (89: 89: 91: 93: 93) sts using 4 ½ mm (US 7) needles.

Work 18 (18: 20: 20: 20: 20) rows in double moss st setting stitches as for long sleeve.

Place a marker at each end of last row.

Cast off 1 st at each end of next row and 4 foll 4th rows.

73 (79: 79: 81: 83: 83) sts.

Place a second set of markers at each end of last row.

Cast off 7 sts at beg of next 2 rows, then 7 (8: 8: 8: 8: 8) at beg of foll 2 rows, and then 8 (9: 9: 9: 9: 9) sts at beg of foll 2 rows.

Place a third set of markers at each end of last row.

Cast off rem 29 (31: 31: 33: 35: 35) sts.

With WS of collar facing RS of garment, matching centre of collar with centre back neck, the markers at each end of cast off edge with shoulder seams and the second set to the corner on each front where stitches of lower collar are cast off, pin and then back stitch the collar in place easing the back neck into collar. Turn the garment and collar so that the collar is now facing the WS of the garment and the seam reversed, and with the rem markers placed halfway across top of lower collar (as in photograph), pin and then backstitch the collar into place.

Join side and sleeve seams.

Set sleeves into armholes.

Sew on buttons to correspond with buttonholes.

Short sleeve

Fold the approx. 6 (6.5: 6.5: 6.5: 7: 7) cm of cuff onto the RS and stitch into place at seam. Sew on button through all layers.

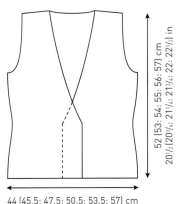

52 [53: 54: 55: 56: 57] cm
20½ [20¾: 21¼: 21½: 22: 22½] in

44 (45.5: 47.5: 50.5: 53.5: 57) cm
17¼ (18: 18¾: 20: 21: 22½) in

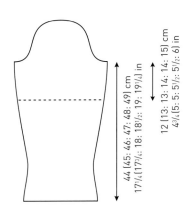

44 (45: 46: 47: 48: 49) cm
17¼ (17¾: 18: 18½: 19: 19¼) in

12 (13: 13: 14: 14: 15) cm
4¾ (5: 5: 5½: 5½: 6) in

Recommendation

Suitable for the knitter with a little experience
Please see pages 10 & 11 for photographs.

	XS	S	M	L	XL	XXL	
To fit	**81**	**86**	**91**	**97**	**102**	**109**	cm
bust	32	34	36	38	40	43	in

Rowan Kid Classic

	12	12	13	14	15	16 x 50gm

Photographed in Smoke

Needles

1 pair 3¾mm (no 9) (US 5) needles
1 pair 4½mm (no 7) (US 7) needles

Tension

21 sts and 27 rows to 10 cm measured over
stocking stitch using 4½mm (US 7) needles.

BILLIE
HOODED WRAP CARDIGAN

BACK

Cast on 101 (107: 111: 117: 123: 131) sts
using 4½mm (US 7) needles.
Beg with a K row, work in st st for 20 rows,
ending with a WS row.
Row 21 (dec) (RS): K2, K2tog, K to last 4 sts,
K2tog tbl, K2.
99 (105: 109: 115: 121: 129) sts.
Working all side seam decreases as set by last
row, dec 1 st at each end of 16th and 4 foll
16th rows.
89 (95: 99: 105: 111: 119) sts.
Cont straight until back measures 54 (54: 55:
55: 55: 55) cm, ending with a WS row.
Shape armholes
Cast off 3 (4: 4: 5: 5: 6) sts at beg of next 2 rows.
83 (87: 91: 95: 101: 107) sts.
Dec 1 st at each end of next 5 (5: 7: 7: 9: 9)
rows, then on foll 2 (3: 2: 3: 3: 5) alt rows,
then on foll 4th row.
67 (69: 71: 73: 75: 77) sts.
Cont straight until armhole measures 18 (19:
19: 20: 21: 22) cm, ending with a WS row.
Shape shoulders and back neck
Cast off 4 sts at beg of next 2 rows.
59 (61: 63: 65: 67: 69) sts.
Next row (RS): Cast off 4 sts, K until there are
9 sts on right needle and turn, leaving rem sts
on a holder.
Work each side of neck separately.
Cast off 4 sts at beg of next row.
Cast off rem 5 sts.
With RS facing, rejoin yarn to rem sts, cast off
centre 33 (35: 37: 39: 41: 43) sts, K to end.
Complete to match first side, reversing
shapings.

Pattern note: When knitting fronts, it is
advisable to join in new balls of yarn at side
seam or armhole edge so that front opening
edge remains neat and tidy as there are no
front opening edgings added afterwards.

LEFT FRONT

Cast on 87 (90: 92: 95: 98: 102) sts using
4½mm (US 7) needles.

Row 1 (RS): Knit.
Row 2: K3, P to end.
These 2 rows set the sts – front opening edge
3 sts in garter st with all other sts in st st.
Keeping sts correct throughout as now set,
work 18 rows, ending with a WS row.
Working all side seam decreases as set by
back, dec 1 st at beg of next and 5 foll
16th rows.
81 (84: 86: 89: 92: 96) sts.
Cont straight until left front matches back to
beg of armhole shaping, ending with a WS row.
Shape armhole
Cast off 3 (4: 4: 5: 5: 6) sts at beg of next row.
78 (80: 82: 84: 87: 90) sts.
Work 1 row.
Dec 1 st at armhole edge of next 5 (5: 7: 7:
9: 9) rows, then on foll 2 (3: 2: 3: 3: 5) alt
rows, then on foll 4th row.
70 (71: 72: 73: 74: 75) sts.
Cont straight until left front matches back
to beg of shoulder shaping, ending with a
WS row.
Shape shoulder
Cast off 4 sts at beg of next and foll alt row,
then 5 sts at beg of foll alt row.
57 (58: 59: 60: 61: 62) sts.
Work 1 row, ending with a WS row.
Shape for hood
Keeping sts correct, cast on 21 (22: 23: 24:
25: 26) sts at beg of next row.
78 (80: 82: 84: 86: 88) sts.
Cont straight until hood section measures
12 (12: 13: 13: 14: 14) cm from cast-on sts,
ending with a WS row.
Dec 1 st at beg of next and foll 12th row, then
on foll 10th row, then on foll 8th row, then on
2 foll 4th rows, then on foll 2 alt rows, then on
foll 5 rows, ending with a WS row.
65 (67: 69: 71: 73: 75) sts.
Cast off 4 sts at beg of next row, 6 sts at beg
of foll alt row, 8 sts at beg of foll alt row, then
12 sts at beg of foll alt row.
35 (37: 39: 41: 43: 45) sts.
Work 1 row, ending with a WS row.
Break yarn and leave sts on a holder.

RIGHT FRONT

Cast on 87 (90: 92: 95: 98: 102) sts using 4½mm (US 7) needles.

Row 1 (RS): Knit.

Row 2: P to last 3 sts, K3.

These 2 rows set the sts – front opening edge 3 sts in garter st with all other sts in st st.

Keeping sts correct throughout as now set, work 18 rows, ending with a WS row.

Working all side seam decreases as set by back, dec 1 st at end of next and 5 foll 16th rows.

81 (84: 86: 89: 92: 96) sts.

Complete to match left front, reversing shapings.

SLEEVES (both alike)

Cast on 65 (67: 69: 71: 73: 75) sts using 3¾mm (US 5) needles.

Row 1 (RS): K1, *P1, K1, rep from * to end.

Row 2: P1, *K1, P1, rep from * to end.

These 2 rows form rib.

Cont in rib, dec 1 st at each end of 5th and 3 foll 6th rows, then on 2 foll 8th rows.

53 (55: 57: 59: 61: 63) sts.

Work in rib for a further 7 rows, ending with a WS row.

Change to 4½mm (US 7) needles.

Beg with a K row, work in st st for 8 rows, ending with a WS row.

Next row (inc) (RS): K3, M1, K to last 3 sts, M1, K3.

55 (57: 59: 61: 63: 65) sts.

Working all increases as set by last row, inc 1 st at each end of 12th (12th: 12th: 12th: 12th: 14th) and every foll 12th (12th: 12th: 12th: 14th: 14th) row to 67 (67: 67: 65: 75: 77) sts, then on every foll - (14th: 14th: 14th: -: -) row until there are - (69: 71: 73: -: -) sts.

Cont straight until sleeve measures 51 (52: 53: 54: 55: 56) cm, ending with a WS row.

Shape top

Cast off 3 (4: 4: 5: 5: 6) sts at beg of next 2 rows.

61 (61: 63: 63: 65: 65) sts.

Dec 1 st at each end of next 3 rows, then on foll alt row, then on 4 (5: 5: 5: 5: 6) foll 4th rows.

45 (43: 45: 45: 47: 45) sts.

Work 1 row.

Dec 1 st at each end of next and every foll alt row until 35 sts rem, then on foll row, ending with a WS row. 33 sts.

Cast off 3 sts at beg of next 2 rows.

Cast off rem 27 sts.

MAKING UP

Press all pieces using a warm iron over a damp cloth.

Join both shoulder seams using back stitch or mattress stitch if preferred.

Join top seam of hood by grafting together the 2 sets of sts left on holders. Join shaped cast-off and row-end edges of hood to form back seam, then sew cast-on edge of hood to back neck. Join side seams. Join sleeve seams, reversing seam for turn-back.

Insert sleeves into armholes.

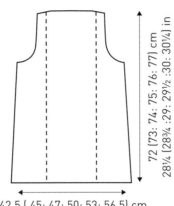

42.5 (45: 47: 50: 53: 56.5) cm
16¾ (17¾ : 18½ : 19½ : 21: 22¼) in

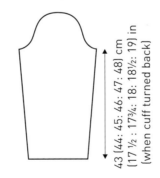

SID

TUNIC WITH DEEP RAGLANS

Recommendation

Suitable for the novice knitter

Please see pages 12 & 13 for photographs.

	XS	S	M	L	XL	XXL	
To fit	**81**	**86**	**91**	**97**	**102**	**109**	cm
bust	32	34	36	38	40	43	in

Rowan Kidsilk Aura

10   12   12   13   14   15 x 25gm

Photographed in Nearly Black

Needles

1 pair 4mm (no 8) (US 6) needles

1 pair 4½mm (no 7) (US 7) needles

1 pair 5mm (no 6) (US 8) needles

1 pair 5½mm (no 5) (US 9) needles

4mm (no 8) (US 6) circular needle

4½mm (no 7) (US 7) circular needle

Tension

15 sts and 20 rows to 10 cm measured over stocking stitch using 5½mm (US 9) needles.

BACK

Cast on 144 (152: 160: 168: 176: 188) sts using 5mm (US 8) needles.

Row 1 (RS): *K2, lift 2nd st on right needle over first st and off right needle, rep from * to end.

72 (76: 80: 84: 88: 94) sts.

Row 2: P0 (1: 0: 1: 0: 0), K1 (2: 1: 2: 1: 0), *P2, K2, rep from * to last 3 (1: 3: 1: 3: 2) sts, P2 (1: 2: 1: 2: 2), K1 (0: 1: 0: 1: 0).

Row 3: K0 (1: 0: 1: 0: 0), P1 (2: 1: 2: 1: 0), *K2, P2, rep from * to last 3 (1: 3: 1: 3: 2) sts, K2 (1: 2: 1: 2: 2), P1 (0: 1: 0: 1: 0).

Last 2 rows form rib.

Work in rib for a further 17 rows, ending with a WS row.

Change to 5½mm (US 9) needles.

Beg with a K row, work in st st until back measures 44 (44: 45: 45: 45: 45) cm, ending with a WS row.

Shape raglan armholes

Cast off 6 sts at beg of next 2 rows.

60 (64: 68: 72: 76: 82) sts.

Work 2 rows.

Next row (dec) (RS): K2, K2tog, K to last 4 sts, K2tog tbl, K2. 58 (62: 66: 70: 74: 80) sts.

Working all raglan armhole decreases as set by last row, dec 1 st at each end of 4th and 10 (9: 8: 7: 7: 5) foll 4th rows, then on foll 0 (3: 5: 8: 9: 14) alt rows. 36 (36: 38: 38: 40: 40) sts.

Work 1 row, ending with a WS row.

Cast off.

FRONT

Work as given for back until 40 (44: 46: 46: 48: 48) sts rem in raglan armhole shaping.

Work 1 (3: 1: 1: 1: 1) rows, ending with a WS row.

Shape neck

XS size only

Next row (RS): K6 and turn, leaving rem sts on a holder. 6 sts.

Work each side of neck separately.

Dec 1 st at beg of next row. 5 sts.

Next row (RS): K2, K3tog. 3 sts.

Dec 1 st at neck edge of next 2 rows. 1 st.

S, M, L, XL and XXL sizes only

Next row (RS): K2, K2tog, K4 and turn, leaving rem sts on a holder. 7 sts.

Work each side of neck separately.

Dec 1 st at neck edge of next 3 rows **and at same time** dec 1 st at raglan armhole edge of 2nd row. 3 sts.

Next row (RS): K3tog. 1 st.

All sizes

Work 1 row, ending with a WS row.

Fasten off.

With RS facing, rejoin yarn to rem sts, cast off centre 28 (28: 30: 30: 32: 32) sts, K to last 0 (4: 4: 4: 4: 4) sts, (K2tog tbl, K2) 0 (1: 1: 1: 1: 1) times. 6 (7: 7: 7: 7: 7) sts.

Complete to match first side, reversing shapings.

SLEEVES (both alike)

Cast on 72 (72: 76: 80: 80: 84) sts using 4½mm (US 7) needles.

Row 1 (RS): *K2, lift 2nd st on right needle over first st and off right needle, rep from * to end.

36 (36: 38: 40: 40: 42) sts.

Change to 4mm (US 6) needles.

Row 2: P0 (0: 0: 1: 1: 0), K1 (1: 2: 2: 2: 0), *P2, K2, rep from * to last 3 (3: 0: 1: 1: 2) sts, P2 (2: 0: 1: 1: 2), K1 (1: 0: 0: 0: 0).

Row 3: K0 (0: 0: 1: 1: 0), P1 (1: 2: 2: 2: 0), *K2, P2, rep from * to last 3 (3: 0: 1: 1: 2) sts, K2 (2: 0: 1: 1: 2), P1 (1: 0: 0: 0: 0).

Last 2 rows form rib.

Work in rib for a further 11 rows, ending with a WS row.

Dec 1 st at each end of next row.

34 (34: 36: 38: 38: 40) sts.

Work 21 (21: 21: 23: 23: 23) rows.

Inc 1 st at each end of next row.

36 (36: 38: 40: 40: 42) sts.

Work 11 rows, ending with a WS row.

Change to 5½mm (US 9) needles.

Next row (inc) (RS): K3 (1: 2: 3: 3: 4), M1, (K2, M1) 15 (17: 17: 17: 17: 17) times, K3 (1: 2: 3: 3: 4).

52 (54: 56: 58: 58: 60) sts.

Beg with a P row, work in st st until sleeve measures 26 (27: 27: 29: 30: 31) cm, ending with a WS row.
Next row (inc) (RS): K3, M1, K to last 3 sts, M1, K3. 54 (56: 58: 60: 60: 62) sts.
Working all increases as set by last row, inc 1 st at each end of 4th and 3 foll 4th rows, then on foll 8 alt rows.
78 (80: 82: 84: 84: 86) sts.
Work 3 rows, ending with a WS row.

Shape raglan
Cast off 6 sts at beg of next 2 rows.
66 (68: 70: 72: 72: 74) sts.
Working all raglan decreases in same way as for back raglan armhole decreases, dec 1 st at each end of 3rd and 4 (5: 4: 5: 6: 7) foll 4th rows, then on foll 13 (12: 14: 13: 12: 11) alt rows.
30 (32: 32: 34: 34: 36) sts.
Work 1 row, ending with a WS row.

Left sleeve only
Next row (RS): K2, K2tog, K12 (13: 13: 14: 14: 15), cast off rem 14 (15: 15: 16: 16: 17) sts.
Rejoin yarn with **WS** facing and cont as folls:
Next row: P to last 4 sts, P2tog, P2.

Right sleeve only
Next row (RS): Cast off 14 (15: 15: 16: 16: 17) sts, K to last 4 sts, K2tog tbl, K2.
Next row: P2, P2tog tbl, P to end.

Both sleeves
Cast off rem 14 (15: 15: 16: 16: 17) sts.

MAKING UP
Pin the pieces out pulling gently into shape and steam gently.
Join all 4 raglan seams using back stitch or mattress stitch if preferred.

Neckband
With RS facing and using 4½mm (US 7) circular needle, pick up and knit 28 (30: 30: 32: 32: 34) sts from top of left sleeve placing marker between centre 2 sts, 40 (38: 42: 40: 44: 42) sts from front, 28 (30: 30: 32: 32: 34) sts from top of right sleeve placing marker between centre 2 sts, then 36 (38: 38: 40: 40: 42) sts from back.
132 (136: 140: 144: 148: 152) sts.
Round 1 (RS): K0 (0: 0: 1: 1: 0), P1 (2: 2: 2: 2: 0), *K2, P2, rep from * to last 3 (2: 2: 1: 1: 0) sts, K2 (2: 2: 1: 1: 0), P1 (0: 0: 0: 0: 0).
This round sets position of rib.
Keeping rib correct, cont as folls:
Work 3 rounds.

Round 5 (dec) (RS): *Rib to within 3 sts of marker, K3tog, slip marker onto right needle, sl 1, K2tog, psso, rep from * once more, rib to end. 124 (128: 132: 136: 140: 144) sts.
Rep last 4 rounds once more.
116 (120: 124: 128: 132: 136) sts.
Work 1 round.
Change to 4mm (US 6) circular needle.
Work 1 round.
Cast off in rib.
Join side and sleeve seams.

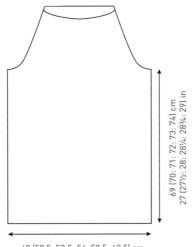

69 (70: 71: 72: 73: 74) cm
27 (27½: 28: 28¼: 28¾: 29) in

48 (50.5: 53.5: 56: 58.5: 62.5) cm
19 (20: 21: 22: 23: 24½) in

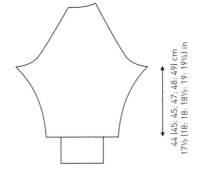

44 (45: 45: 47: 48: 49) cm
17½ (18: 18: 18½: 19: 19¼) in

Recommendation

Suitable for the knitter with little experience
Please see pages 18, 19 & 34 for photographs.

	XS	S	M	L	XL	XXL	
To fit	**81**	**86**	**91**	**97**	**102**	**107**	**cm**
bust	32	34	36	38	40	42	in

Rowan Wool Cotton

	9	10	10	11	12	12	x 50gm

Rowan Felted Tweed

	6	6	7	7	7	8	x 50gm

Photographed in Inky (Wool Cotton) & Carbon
(Felted Tweed)

Needles

1 pair 3 ¼ mm (no 10) (US 3) needles
1 pair 3 ¾ mm (no 9) (US 5) needles

Buttons – 5

Tension

23 sts and 32 rows to 10 cm measured over
stocking stitch using 3 ¾ mm (US 5) needles.

Special abbreviation

MP = Make picot: cast on 1 st, cast off 1 st.
(See information page for details)

MAGGIE
CARDIGAN WITH CURVED FRONTS & GARTER STITCH TRIM

BACK
Lower back edging
Cast on 27 (27: 28: 28: 29: 29) sts using
3 ¼ mm (US 3) needles and work as folls:
Knit 2 rows.

Next row (RS): MP, K until there are 7 sts on
RH needle, wrap next st, turn and K to end.

Next row: MP, K until there are 14 sts on RH
needle, wrap next st, turn and K to end.

Next row: MP, K until there are 21 sts on RH
needle, wrap next st, turn and K to end.

Working a picot at beg of every RS row as set,
work a further 148 (160: 172: 184: 196: 208)
rows, ending with a WS row.

Next row (RS): MP, K until there are 21 sts
on RH needle, wrap next st, turn and K to end.

Next row: MP, K until there are 14 sts on RH
needle, wrap next st, turn and K to end.

Next row: MP, K until there are 7 sts on RH
needle, wrap next st, turn and K to end.

Knit 2 rows.

Cast off, but do not break yarn.

Upper back
With RS facing and using 3 ¾ mm (US 5)
needles, pick up and knit 87 (93: 99: 105:
111: 117) sts along straight edge of border
and cont as folls:

Beg with a P row, work 7 rows in stocking st,
ending with a WS row.

Next row (RS)(inc): K3, M1, K to last 3 sts,
M1, K3.

89 (95: 101: 107: 113: 119) sts.

Working all incs as set by last row, inc 1 st at
each end of 2 foll 8th rows, then on every foll
10th row until there are 99 (105: 111: 117:
123: 129) sts.

Cont straight until back measures 20 (20: 21:
21: 22: 22) cm from pick-up row, ending with
a WS row.

Shape raglan
Cast off 4 (5: 6: 7: 8: 9) sts at beg of next
2 rows. 91 (95: 99: 103: 107: 111) sts.

Next row (RS)(dec): K1, K2tog, K to last 3 sts,
K2tog tbl, K1.

Next row (WS)(dec): P1, P2tog tbl, P to last
3 sts, P2tog, P1.

Working all decs as set by last 2 rows, dec
1 st at each end of next 3 (3: 7: 7: 9: 9) rows,
then on every foll alt row until 31 (33: 33:
33: 35: 35) sts rem, ending with a RS row.

Dec 1 st at each end of next row, ending with
a WS row.

Cast off rem 29 (31: 31: 31: 33: 33) sts.

LEFT FRONT
Lower edging
Cast on 27 (27: 28: 28: 29: 29) sts using
3 ¼ mm (US 3) needles and work as folls:

Next row (RS): Knit.

Next row: MP, K to end.

Next row: Knit.

Shape side edge
Next row (WS): MP, K until there are 7 sts
on RH needle, wrap next st, turn and K to end.

Next row: MP, K until there are 14 sts on RH
needle, wrap next st, turn and K to end.

Next row: MP, K until there are 21 sts on RH
needle, wrap next st, turn and K to end.

Working a picot at beg of every WS row as set,
work a further 31 (37: 41: 47: 51: 57) rows,
ending with a WS row.

Shape front edge
Next row (RS): K to last 3 sts, K2tog tbl, K1.

Working all decs as set by last row, and
keeping picot edging correct, cont as folls:

Work 9 rows straight, ending with a WS row.

Dec 1 st at end of next row, then on foll 8th
row, then on foll 6th row, then on foll 4th row.
22 (22: 23: 23: 24: 24) sts.

Work 1 row, ending with a WS row.

Dec 1 st at end of next row and every foll alt
row until 11 sts rem.

Next row (WS): MP, K2tog, K to end.

Working all decs as set, dec 1 st on shaped
edge of every row until 6 sts rem.

Next row (RS): K2, K3tog tbl, K1.

Next row: MP, K3tog. 2 sts. Cast off.

Upper left front
With RS facing and using 3 ¾ mm (US 5)
needles, pick up and knit 51 (54: 57: 60:
63: 66) sts along straight edge of border
and cont as folls:

Next row (WS): MP, K until there are 12 sts on RH needle, P to end.

Next row: K to end.

Working a picot on every **alt** WS row as set, and keeping 12 sts at front opening edge in garter st with picot edging for button border, cont in patt, work 5 rows without shaping, ending with a WS row.

Next row (RS)(inc): K3, M1, K to end. 52 (55: 58: 61: 64: 67) sts.

Working all incs as set by last row, cont in patt as set, inc 1 st at beg of 2 foll 8th rows, then on every foll 10th row until there are 57 (60: 63: 66: 69: 72) sts.

Cont straight until left front measures same as back to beg of raglan armhole shaping, measuring from pick-up row, ending with a WS row.

Shape raglan

Cast off 4 (5: 6: 7: 8: 9) sts at beg of next row. 53 (55: 57: 59: 61: 63) sts.

Work 1 row.

Next row (RS)(dec): K1, K2tog, K to end.

Next row (WS)(dec): MP, K until there are 12 sts on RH needle, P to last 3 sts, P2tog, P1.

Working all decs as set by last 2 rows, dec 1 st at armhole edge of next 3 (3: 7: 7: 9: 9) rows, then on every foll alt row until 41 (44: 44: 44: 47: 47) sts rem, ending with a RS row.

Next row (WS): MP, K until there are 13 sts on RH needle, P to end.

Next row: K1, K2tog, K to end.

Rep last 2 rows once more.

Next row (WS): MP, K until there are 14 sts on RH needle, P to end.

Next row: K1, K2tog, K to end.

Rep last 2 rows once more.

Next row (WS): MP, K until there are 15 sts on RH needle, P to end.

Taking an extra st into the garter st border every 4 rows as set, cont in patt, shaping raglan by dec 1 st at armhole edge on every foll alt row until 23 (24: 24: 24: 25: 25) sts rem, then on foll row, ending with a WS row.

Leave sts on a holder for neck border.

Mark the positions of 5 buttons on left front, the first on 2nd row of upper front, the last one 6 rows below start of shaped garter st, and rem buttons spaced evenly between.

RIGHT FRONT

Lower edging

Cast on 27 (27: 28: 28: 29: 29) sts using 3 ¼ mm (US 3) needles and work as folls: Knit 2 rows, ending with a WS row.

Shape side edge

Next row (RS): MP, K until there are 7 sts on RH needle, wrap next st, turn and K to end.

Next row: MP, K until there are 14 sts on RH needle, wrap next st, turn and K to end.

Next row: MP, K until there are 21 sts on RH needle, wrap next st, turn and K to end.

Working a picot at beg of every **RS** row as set, work a further 32 (38: 42: 48: 52: 58) rows, ending with a WS row.

Shape front edge

Next row (RS): MP, K2tog, K to end.

Working all decs as set by last row, and keeping picot edging correct, cont as folls: Work 9 rows straight, ending with a WS row.

Dec 1 st at beg of next row, then on foll 8th row, then on foll 6th row, then on foll 4th row.

22 (22: 23: 23: 24: 24) sts.

Work 1 row, ending with a WS row.

Dec 1 st at beg of next row and every foll alt row until 11 sts rem.

Next row (WS): K to last 3 sts, K2tog tbl, K1.

Working all decs as set, dec 1 st on shaped edge of every row until 6 sts rem.

Next row (RS): MP, K3tog, K2.

Next row: K1, K3tog tbl. 2 sts.

Cast off, but do not break yarn.

Upper right front

With RS facing and using 3 ¾ mm (US 5) needles, pick up and knit 51 (54: 57: 60: 63: 66) sts along straight edge of border and cont as folls:

Next row (WS): P to last 12 sts, K to end.

Next row (RS)(buttonhole row): MP, K until there are 5 sts on RH needle, cast off 3 sts, K to end.

Next row: P to last 12 sts, K to end, casting-on 3 sts over those cast-off on previous row.

Working a further 4 buttonholes to correspond with positions marked for buttons, complete to match left front, reversing all shapings and working a picot on every **alt RS** row.

SLEEVES

Cuff (knitted from side to side)

Cast on 14 (14: 15: 15: 16: 16) sts using 3 ¼ mm (US 3) needles and work as folls: Knit 1 row.

Next row (WS): K until there are 4 sts on RH needle, wrap next st, turn and K to end.

Next row: K until there are 8 sts on RH needle, wrap next st, turn and K to end.

Knit 1 row, ending with a WS row.

Working a picot at beg of every RS row, work a further 67 (67: 71: 71: 75: 75) rows in garter st, ending with a RS row.

Next row: K until there are 8 sts on RH needle, wrap next st, turn and K to end.

Next row: K until there are 4 sts on RH needle, wrap next st, turn and K to end.

Knit 1 row, ending with a WS row.

Cast off, but do not break yarn.

Upper sleeve

With RS facing and using 3 ¾ mm (US 5) needles, pick up and knit 51 (51: 53: 53: 55: 55) sts along straight edge of cuff.

Beg with a P row, work 9 rows in stocking st, ending with a WS row.

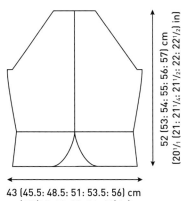

52 [53: 54: 55: 56: 57] cm
(20½: [21: 21¼: 21½: 22: 22½] in)

43 [45.5: 48.5: 51: 53.5: 56] cm
[17 (18: 19: 20: 21: 22) in]

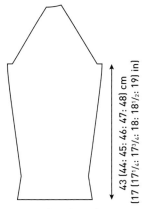

43 (44: 45: 46: 47: 48) cm
(17 [17¼: 17¾: 18: 18½: 19] in)

Continued on next page...

Recommendation
Suitable for the novice knitter
Please see pages 38, 46 & 47 for photographs.

One size

Rowan Cashsoft Aran
2 x 50gm
Plus contrast colour for pompom
Photographed in Black with Redwood 4 ply cashsoft & Thunder with Black 4 ply cashsoft

Needles
1 pair 3¾mm (no 9) (US 5) needles
1 pair 4½mm (no 7) (US 7) needles

Tension
19 sts and 25 rows to 10 cm measured over stocking stitch using 4½mm (US 7) needles.

LUCKY
TEXTURED BERET WITH CONTRAST POMPOM

BERET
Cast on 90 sts using 3¾mm (US 5) needles.
Row 1 (RS): K1, *K2, P2, rep from * to last st, K1.
Row 2: P1, *K2, P2, rep from * to last st, P1.
These 2 rows form rib.
Work in rib for a further 8 rows, end with a WS row.
Change to 4½mm (US 7) needles.
Cont in patt as folls:
Row 1 (RS): P1, *K1 tbl, P3, M1, rep from * to last st, P1. 112 sts.
Row 2 and every foll alt row: Knit.
Row 3: P1, *K1 tbl, P4, rep from * to last st, P1.
Row 5: P1, *K1 tbl, P4, M1, rep from * to last st, P1. 134 sts.
Row 7: P1, *K1 tbl, P5, rep from * to last st, P1.
Row 9: P1, *K1 tbl, P5, M1, rep from * to last st, P1. 156 sts.
Row 11: P1, *K1 tbl, P6, rep from * to last st, P1.
Rows 13, 15, 17, 19 and 21: As row 11.
Row 23: P1, *K1 tbl, P6, K1 tbl, P4, P2tog, rep from * to last st, P1. 145 sts.
Row 25: P1, *K1 tbl, P6, K1 tbl, P5, rep from * to last st, P1.
Row 27: P1, *K1 tbl, P6, K1 tbl, P3, P2tog, rep from * to last st, P1. 134 sts.
Row 29: P1, *K1 tbl, P6, K1 tbl, P4, rep from * to last st, P1.
Row 31: P1, *K1 tbl, P6, K1 tbl, P2, P2tog, rep from * to last st, P1. 123 sts.

Row 33: P1, *K1 tbl, P6, K1 tbl, P3, rep from * to last st, P1.
Row 35: P1, *K1 tbl, P6, K1 tbl, P1, P2tog, rep from * to last st, P1. 112 sts.
Row 37: P1, *K1 tbl, P6, K1 tbl, P2tog, rep from * to last st, P1. 101 sts.
Row 39: P1, *K1 tbl, P6, P2tog, rep from * to last st, P1. 90 sts.
Row 41: P1, *K1 tbl, P5, P2tog, rep from * to last st, P1. 79 sts.
Row 43: P1, *K1 tbl, P4, P2tog, rep from * to last st, P1. 68 sts.
Row 45: P1, *K1 tbl, P3, P2tog, rep from * to last st, P1. 57 sts.
Row 47: P1, *K1 tbl, P2, P2tog, rep from * to last st, P1. 46 sts.
Row 49: P1, *K1 tbl, P1, P2tog, rep from * to last st, P1. 35 sts.
Row 51: P1, *K1 tbl, P2tog, rep from * to last st, P1. 24 sts.
Row 52: Knit.
Break yarn and thread through rem 24 sts.
Pull up tight and fasten off securely.

MAKING UP
Join back seam, preferably using mattress stitch.
Using contrast yarn, make a 5 cm diameter pompom and attach to top of beret.

Maggie – Continued from previous page...

Next row (RS)(inc): K3, M1, K to last 3 sts, M1, K3. 53 (53: 55: 55: 57: 57) sts.
Working all incs as set by last row, cont in st st, inc 1 st at each end of every 10th (10th: 10th: 8th: 8th: 8th) row to 65 (73: 73: 71: 71: 79) sts, then on every foll 12th (-: 12th: 10th: 10th: 10th) row to 71 (-: 75: 79: 81: 83) sts.
Cont straight until sleeve measures 37 (38: 38.5: 39.5: 40: 41) cm from pick-up row, ending with a WS row.
Shape raglan
Cast off 4 (5: 6: 7: 8: 9) sts at beg of next 2 rows. 63 (63: 63: 65: 65: 65) sts.

Work 2 rows straight, ending with a WS row.
Working all decs as given for back raglan shaping, dec 1 st at each end of next row and 1 (2: 1: 3: 3: 5) foll 4th rows, then on every foll alt row until 11 sts rem, ending with a **RS** row.
Work 1 row, ending with a WS row.
Cast off rem 11 sts.

MAKING UP
Press as described on information page.
Join raglan seams using backstitch or mattress stitch if preferred.

Neckband
With RS facing and using 3 ¼ mm (US 3) needles, patt across 22 (23: 23: 23: 24: 24) sts from right front, pick up and knit 9 sts from top of right sleeve, 29 (31: 31: 31: 33: 33) sts from back, 9 sts from top of left sleeve, then patt across 22 (23: 23: 23: 24: 24) sts from left front.
91 (95: 95: 95: 99: 99) sts.
Patt 8 (8: 8: 10: 10: 10) rows.
Cast off knitwise.
Join side and sleeve seams. Sew on buttons to correspond with buttonholes.

LAUREN

TEXTURED CARDIGAN WITH DEEP RAGLANS

Recommendation

Suitable for the knitter with a little experience
Please see pages 20 & 21 for photographs.

	XS	S	M	L	XL	XXL	
To fit	**81**	**86**	**91**	**97**	**102**	**109**	cm
bust	32	34	36	38	40	43	in

Rowan Cashsoft 4 ply

	9	9	10	10	11	12 x 50gm

Photographed in Black

Needles

1 pair 2¼mm (no 13) (US 1) needles
1 pair 3mm (no 11) (US 2/3) needles

Buttons – 12

Tension

30 sts and 39 rows to 10 cm measured over
pattern using 3mm (US 2/3) needles.

Special abbreviation

cluster 2 = yrn, P2, lift the yrn over these 2 sts
and off right needle.

BACK

Cast on 145 (153: 161: 169: 175: 187) sts
using 2¼mm (US 1) needles.
Row 1 (RS): K1, *P1, K1, rep from * to end.
Row 2: P1, *K1, P1, rep from * to end.
These 2 rows form rib.
Work in rib for a further 14 (14: 14: 18:
18: 18) rows, ending with a WS row.
Next row (dec) (RS): Rib 4, sl 1, K1, psso,
slip st now on right needle back onto left
needle and lift 2nd st on left needle over this
st, then slip st back onto right needle – 2 sts
decreased, rib to last 7 sts, sl 1, K2tog, psso
– 2 sts decreased, rib 4.
141 (149: 157: 165: 171: 183) sts.
Working all decreases as set by last row, dec
2 sts at each end of 8th and 4 foll 8th rows.
121 (129: 137: 145: 151: 163) sts.
Work 3 rows, inc 1 st at end of last row and
ending with a WS row.
122 (130: 138: 146: 152: 164) sts.
Change to 3mm (US 2/3) needles.
Now work in patt as folls:
Row 1 (RS): Knit.
Row 2: Purl.
Row 3: Knit.
Row 4: P6 (4: 2: 6: 3: 3), cluster 2, *P4,
cluster 2, rep from * to last 6 (4: 2: 6: 3: 3) sts,
P6 (4: 2: 6: 3: 3).
Rows 5 to 8: As rows 1 and 2, twice.
Row 9: Knit.
Row 10: P3 (1: 5: 3: 6: 6), cluster 2, *P4,
cluster 2, rep from * to last 3 (1: 5: 3: 6: 6) sts,
P3 (1: 5: 3: 6: 6).
Rows 11 and 12: As rows 1 and 2.
These 12 rows form patt.
Keeping patt correct, cont as folls:
Work 2 rows, ending with a WS row.
Next row (inc) (RS): K2, M1, patt to last 2 sts,
M1, K2.
Working all increases as set by last row, inc 1 st
at each end of 6th and 5 foll 6th rows, taking extra
sts into patt. 136 (144: 152: 160: 166: 178) sts.
Cont straight until back measures approx 28
(29: 29: 30: 30: 31) cm, ending after a cluster
patt row and with a WS row.

Shape raglan armholes

Keeping patt correct, cast off 5 sts at beg
of next 2 rows.
126 (134: 142: 150: 156: 168) sts.
Work 2 (2: 2: 0: 0: 0) rows.
Dec 1 st at each end of next 1 (1: 1: 3:
3: 11) rows, then on 5 (2: 2: 0: 0: 0)
foll 4th rows, then on foll 41 (47: 49:
53: 55: 51) alt rows.
32 (34: 38: 38: 40: 44) sts.
Work 1 row, ending with a WS row.
Cast off.

LEFT FRONT

Cast on 82 (86: 90: 94: 96: 102) sts using
2¼mm (US 1) needles.
Row 1 (RS): *K1, P1, rep from * to last 8 sts,
P8 (for front band).
Row 2: K8 (for front band), *K1, P1, rep
from * to end.
Row 3: *K1, P1, rep from * to last 8 sts, K8
(for front band).
Row 4: P8 (for front band), *K1, P1, rep
from * to end.
These 4 rows set the sts – front opening
8 sts in ridge st (for front band) with all
other sts in rib.
Cont as set for a further 12 (12: 12:
16: 16: 16) rows, ending with a WS row.
Working all side seam decreases as set
by back, dec 2 sts at beg of next and 5 foll
6th rows.
70 (74: 78: 82: 84: 90) sts.
Work 3 rows, inc 0 (0: 0: 0: 1: 1) st at end
of last row and ending with a WS row.
70 (74: 78: 82: 85: 91) sts.
Change to 3mm (US 2/3) needles.
Now work in patt as folls:
Row 1 (RS): K to last 9 sts, P1, patt 8 sts.
Row 2: Patt 8 sts, K1, P to end.
Row 3: As row 1.
Row 4: Patt 8 sts, K1, P5, cluster 2, *P4,
cluster 2, rep from * to last 6 (4: 2: 6: 3: 3) sts,
P6 (4: 2: 6: 3: 3).
Rows 5 to 8: As rows 1 and 2, twice.
Row 9: As row 1.

Row 10: Patt 8 sts, K1, P2, cluster 2, *P4, cluster 2, rep from * to last 3 (1: 5: 3: 6: 6) sts, P3 (1: 5: 3: 6: 6).

Rows 11 and 12: As rows 1 and 2.

These 12 rows set the sts – front band 8 sts still in ridge patt, next st in rev st st and rem sts in textured patt as given for back.

Keeping sts correct, cont as folls:

Work 2 rows, ending with a WS row.

Working all side seam increases as set by back, inc 1 st at beg of next and 6 foll 6th rows, taking extra sts into patt.

77 (81: 85: 89: 92: 98) sts.

Cont straight until left front matches back to beg of raglan armhole shaping, ending with a WS row.

Shape raglan armhole

Keeping patt correct, cast off 5 sts at beg of next row. 72 (76: 80: 84: 87: 93) sts.

Work 3 (3: 3: 1: 1: 1) rows.

Dec 1 st at raglan armhole edge of next 1 (1: 1: 3: 3: 11) rows, then on 5 (2: 2: 0: 0: 0) foll 4th rows, then on foll 28 (34: 36: 38: 40: 36) alt rows.

38 (39: 41: 43: 44: 46) sts.

Work 1 row, ending with a WS row.

Shape neck

Next row (RS): K2tog, patt 17 (17: 17: 21: 21: 21) sts and turn, leaving rem 19 (20: 22: 20: 21: 23) sts on a holder.

Keeping patt correct, dec 1 st at neck edge of next 6 rows, then on foll 3 (3: 3: 5: 5: 5) alt rows **and at same time** dec 1 st at raglan armhole edge of 2nd and foll 5 (5: 5: 7: 7: 7) alt rows. 3 sts.

Work 1 row, ending with a WS row.

Next row (RS): sl 1, K2tog, psso.

Next row: P1 and fasten off.

Mark positions for 12 buttons along left front opening edge as folls: lowest 5 buttons on rows 11, 23, 35, 47 and 59 of rib section, top button just below neck shaping, and rem 6 buttons evenly spaced between.

RIGHT FRONT

Cast on 82 (86: 90: 94: 96: 102) sts using 2¼mm (US 1) needles.

Row 1 (RS): P8 (for front band), *P1, K1, rep from * to end.

Row 2: *P1, K1, rep from * to last 8 sts, K8 (for front band).

Row 3: K8 (for front band), *P1, K1, rep from * to end.

Row 4: *P1, K1, rep from * to last 8 sts, P8 (for front band).

These 4 rows set the sts – front opening 8 sts in ridge st (for front band) with all other sts in rib. Cont as set for a further 6 rows, ending with a WS row.

Row 11 (buttonhole row) (RS): Patt 3 sts, cast off 2 sts (to make a buttonhole – cast on 2 sts over these cast-off sts on next row), patt to end.

Working a further 11 buttonholes in this way to correspond with positions marked for buttons on left front and noting that no further reference will be made to buttonholes, cont as folls:

Cont as set for a further 5 (5: 5: 9: 9: 9) rows, ending with a WS row.

Working all side seam decreases as set by back, dec 2 sts at end of next and 5 foll 6th rows.

70 (74: 78: 82: 84: 90) sts.

Work 3 rows, inc 0 (0: 0: 0: 1: 1) st at beg of last row and ending with a WS row.

70 (74: 78: 82: 85: 91) sts.

Change to 3mm (US 2/3) needles.

Now work in patt as folls:

Row 1 (RS): Patt 8 sts, P1, K to end.

Row 2: P to last 9 sts, K1, patt 8 sts.

Row 3: As row 1.

Row 4: P6 (4: 2: 6: 3: 3), cluster 2, *P4, cluster 2, rep from * to last 14 sts, P5, K1, patt 8 sts.

Rows 5 to 8: As rows 1 and 2, twice.

Row 9: As row 1.

Row 10: P3 (1: 5: 3: 6: 6), cluster 2, *P4, cluster 2, rep from * to last 11 sts, P2, K1, patt 8 sts.

Rows 11 and 12: As rows 1 and 2.

These 12 rows set the sts – front band 8 sts still in ridge patt, next st in rev st st and rem sts in textured patt as given for back.

Keeping sts correct, complete to match left front, reversing shapings and working first row of neck shaping as folls:

Next row (RS): Patt 19 (20: 22: 20: 21: 23) sts and slip these sts onto a holder, patt to last 2 sts, K2tog.

18 (18: 18: 22: 22: 22) sts.

SLEEVES (both alike)

Cast on 77 (79: 83: 85: 89: 91) sts using 2¼mm (US 1) needles.

Work in rib as given for back for 10 (10: 10: 14: 14: 14) rows, ending with a WS row.

Inc 1 st at each end of next and 2 foll 10th rows, taking inc sts into rib.

83 (85: 89: 91: 95: 97) sts.

Work a further 4 rows, ending with a **RS** row.

Next row (inc) (WS): Rib 5 (6: 5: 6: 5: 6), M1, *rib 12 (12: 13: 13: 14: 14), M1, rep from * 5 times more, rib 6 (7: 6: 7: 6: 7).

90 (92: 96: 98: 102: 104) sts.

Change to 3mm (US 2/3) needles.

Now work in patt as folls:

Row 1 (RS): Knit.

Row 2: Purl.

Row 3: Knit.

Row 4: P2 (3: 5: 6: 2: 3), cluster 2, *P4, cluster 2, rep from * to last 2 (3: 5: 6: 2: 3) sts, P2 (3: 5: 6: 2: 3).

Row 5: K2, M1, K to last 2 sts, M1, K2.

92 (94: 98: 100: 104: 106) sts.

Row 6: Purl.

Rows 7 and 8: As rows 1 and 2.

Row 9: As row 5.

94 (96: 100: 102: 106: 108) sts.

Row 10: P7 (2: 4: 5: 7: 2), cluster 2, *P4, cluster 2, rep from * to last 7 (2: 4: 5: 7: 2) sts, P7 (2: 4: 5: 7: 2).

Rows 11 and 12: As rows 1 and 2.

These 12 rows form patt and start sleeve shaping.

Working all increases as set by row 5, cont in patt, shaping sides by inc 1 st at each end of next and 10 foll 4th rows, then on foll 16 alt rows, taking inc sts into patt.

148 (150: 154: 156: 160: 162) sts.

Work 3 rows, ending after a cluster patt row and with a WS row.

Shape raglan

Keeping patt correct, cast off 5 sts at beg of next 2 rows. 138 (140: 144: 146: 150: 152) sts.

Dec 1 st at each end of next 5 (7: 7: 9: 9: 11) rows, then on every foll alt row until 38 sts rem.

Work 1 row, ending with a WS row.

Left sleeve only

Dec 1 st at each end of next row, then cast off 4 sts at beg of foll row. 32 sts.

Dec 1 st at beg of next row, then cast off 5 sts at beg of foll row. 26 sts.

Rep last 2 rows once more. 20 sts.

Dec 1 st at beg of next row, then cast off 6 sts at beg of foll row. 13 sts.

Right sleeve only

Cast off 5 sts at beg and dec 1 st at end of next row. 32 sts.

Work 1 row.

Rep last 2 rows twice more. 20 sts.
Cast off 6 sts at beg and dec 1 st at end
of next row. 13 sts.
Work 1 row.
Both sleeves
Rep last 2 rows once more.
Cast off rem 6 sts.

MAKING UP
Press all pieces using a warm iron over a
damp cloth.
Join all 4 raglan seams using back stitch
or mattress stitch if preferred.
Neckband
With RS facing and using 2¼mm (US 1)
needles, slip 19 (20: 22: 20: 21: 23) sts from
right front holder onto right needle, rejoin yarn
and pick up and knit 16 (16: 16: 20: 20: 20)
sts up right side of neck, 28 sts from top of
right sleeve, 32 (34: 38: 38: 40: 44) sts from
back, 28 sts from top of left sleeve, and 16
(16: 16: 20: 20: 20) sts down left side of neck,
then patt 19 (20: 22: 20: 21: 23) sts from left
front holder.
158 (162: 170: 174: 178: 186) sts.
Beg with a K row, work in rev st st for 4 rows,
ending with a **RS** row.
Cast off knitwise (on **WS**).
Join side and sleeve seams. Sew on buttons.

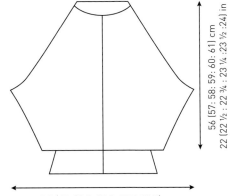

56 (57: 58: 59: 60: 61) cm
22 (22 ½ : 22 ¾ : 23 ¼ :23 ½ :24) in

45.5 (48: 50.5: 53.5: 55.5: 59.5) cm
18 (19: 20: 21: 22: 23½) in

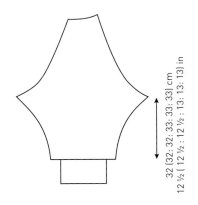

32 (32: 32: 32: 33: 33) cm
12 ½ (12 ½ : 12 ½ : 13: 13: 13) in

JEN
PRETTY CROPPED CARDIGAN

Recommendation

Suitable for the novice knitter
Please see pages 22 & 24 for photographs.

	XS	S	M	L	XL	XXL	
To fit	**81**	**86**	**91**	**97**	**102**	**109**	cm
bust	32	34	36	38	40	43	in

Rowan Bamboo Soft

| 5 | 6 | 6 | 7 | 7 | 8 x 50gm |

Photographed in Black

Needles

1 pair 3mm (no 11) (US 2/3) needles
1 pair 3¾mm (no 9) (US 5) needles

Buttons – 9

Tension

Before steaming: 24 sts and 30 rows to
10 cm measured over stocking stitch using
3¾mm (US 5) needles.

Tension note: The Bamboo Soft yarn relaxes
after steaming. This opens the knitting and
changes the tension by approximately one
stitch in the width but does not affect the rows
(23 sts and 30 rows). Therefore your knitting,
before steaming, should have a tension of
24 sts and 30 rows to 10 cm. Allowances
have been made within the pattern for this
change (see size diagram for after relaxing
measurements).

BACK

Cast on 79 (85: 91: 97: 103: 111) sts using
3mm (US 2/3) needles.
Row 1 (RS): K1, *P1, K1, rep from * to end.
Row 2: P1, *K1, P1, rep from * to end.
These 2 rows form rib.
Work in rib for a further 14 rows, ending with
a WS row.
Inc 1 st at each end of next and foll 14th row.
83 (89: 95: 101: 107: 115) sts.
Work 3 (5: 5: 7: 7: 9) rows, ending with a
WS row.
Change to 3¾mm (US 5) needles.
Beg with a K row, work in st st for 10 (8: 10:
8: 10: 6) rows, ending with a WS row.
Next row (inc) (RS): K2, M1, K to last 2 sts,
M1, K2. 85 (91: 97: 103: 109: 117) sts.
Working increases as set by last row, inc 1 st
at each end of 14th (14th: 16th: 16th: 18th:
16th) row. 87 (93: 99: 105: 111: 119) sts.
Work 11 (9: 9: 9: 9: 11) rows, ending with
a WS row.
Shape raglan armholes
Cast off 4 sts at beg of next 2 rows.
79 (85: 91: 97: 103: 111) sts.
Work 2 (2: 2: 2: 0: 0) rows.
XXL size only
Next row (dec) (RS): K1, K2tog, K to last 3 sts,
K2tog tbl, K1.
Next row: P1, P2tog tbl, P to last 3 sts, P2tog,
P1. 107 sts.
All sizes
Next row (dec) (RS): K1, K2tog, K to last 3 sts,
K2tog tbl, K1.
77 (83: 89: 95: 101: 105) sts.
Working all raglan armhole decreases as set
by last row, dec 1 st at each end of 4th (4th:
4th: 4th: 2nd: 2nd) and 5 (4: 2: 1: 0: 0) foll
4th rows, then on foll 6 (10: 14: 17: 21: 22)
alt rows. 53 (53: 55: 57: 57: 59) sts.
Work 1 row, ending with a WS row.
Cast off.

LEFT FRONT

Cast on 43 (46: 49: 52: 55: 59) sts using
3mm (US 2/3) needles.

Row 1 (RS): *K1, P1, rep from * to last
7 (6: 7: 6: 7: 7) sts, K1 (0: 1: 0: 1: 1), P6
(for front band).
Row 2: K6 (for front band), P1 (0: 1: 0: 1: 1),
*K1, P1, rep from * to end.
Row 3: *K1, P1, rep from * to last
7 (6: 7: 6: 7: 7) sts, K1 (0: 1: 0: 1: 1),
K6 (for front band).
Row 4: P6 (for front band), P1 (0: 1: 0: 1: 1),
*K1, P1, rep from * to end.
These 4 rows set the sts – front opening edge
6 sts in ridge patt (for front band) with all
other sts in rib.
Cont as set for a further 12 rows, ending with
a WS row.
Inc 1 st at beg of next and foll 14th row.
45 (48: 51: 54: 57: 61) sts.
Work 3 (5: 5: 7: 7: 9) rows, ending with
a WS row.
Change to 3¾mm (US 5) needles.
Next row (RS): K to last 6 sts, patt 6 sts.
Next row: Patt 6 sts, P to end.
These 2 rows set the sts – front opening edge
6 sts still in ridge patt (for front band) with all
other sts now in st st.
Cont as set for a further 8 (6: 8: 6: 8: 4) rows,
ending with a WS row.
Working increases as set by back, inc 1 st
at beg of next and foll 14th (14th: 16th:
16th: 18th: 16th) row.
47 (50: 53: 56: 59: 63) sts.
Work 11 (9: 9: 9: 9: 11) rows, ending with
a WS row.
Shape raglan armholes
Keeping sts correct, cast off 4 sts at beg
of next row.
43 (46: 49: 52: 55: 59) sts.
Work 3 (3: 3: 3: 1: 1) rows.
Working all raglan armhole decreases as set
by back, dec 1 st at raglan armhole edge of
next 1 (1: 1: 1: 1: 3) rows, then on 4 (4: 3: 2:
0: 0) foll 4th rows, then on foll 0 (0: 3: 5: 10:
10) alt rows.
38 (41: 42: 44: 44: 46) sts.
Work 1 (3: 1: 1: 1: 1) rows, ending after ridge
patt row 4 and with a WS row.

Shape neck

Next row (RS): (K1, K2tog) 0 (1: 1: 1: 1: 1) times, K13 (14: 14: 16: 16: 18) and turn, leaving rem 25 (24: 25: 25: 25: 25) sts on a holder. 13 (16: 16: 18: 18: 20) sts.
Dec 1 st at neck edge of next 6 rows, then on foll 1 (2: 2: 3: 3: 4) alt rows **and at same time** dec 1 st at raglan armhole edge of 2nd and 1 (0: 0: 0: 0: 0) foll 4th row, then on foll 1 (4: 4: 5: 5: 6) alt rows. 3 sts.
Work 1 row, ending with a WS row.
Next row (RS): sl 1, K2tog, psso.
Next row: P1 and fasten off.

RIGHT FRONT

Cast on 43 (46: 49: 52: 55: 59) sts using 3mm (US 2/3) needles.
Row 1 (RS): P6 (for front band), K1 (0: 1: 0: 1: 1), *P1, K1, rep from * to end.
Row 2: *P1, K1, rep from * to last 7 (6: 7: 6: 7: 7) sts, P1 (0: 1: 0: 1: 1), K6 (for front band).

XS, S, M and L sizes only

Row 3 (buttonhole row): K2, K2tog, yfwd (to make first buttonhole), K2 (6 sts for front band), K1 (0: 1: 0: -: -), *P1, K1, rep from * to end.
Row 4: *P1, K1, rep from * to last 7 (6: 7: 6: -: -) sts, P1 (0: 1: 0: -: -), P6 (for front band).
These 4 rows set the sts – front opening edge 6 sts in ridge patt (for front band) with all other sts in rib.

XL and XXL sizes only

Row 3: K6 (for front band), K- (-: -: -: 1: 1), *P1, K1, rep from * to end.
Row 4: *P1, K1, rep from * to last - (-: -: -: 7: 7) sts, P - (-: -: -: 1: 1), P6 (for front band).
These 4 rows set the sts – front opening edge 6 sts in ridge patt (for front band) with all other sts in rib.
Work 2 rows.
Row 7 (buttonhole row) (RS): K2, K2tog, yfwd (to make first buttonhole), K2 (6 sts for front band), rib to end.

All sizes

Making a further 7 buttonholes in this way on every foll 12th row from previous buttonhole and noting that no further reference will be made to buttonholes, cont as folls:
Cont as set for a further 12 (12: 12: 12: 9: 9) rows, ending with a WS row.
Inc 1 st at end of next and foll 14th row.
45 (48: 51: 54: 57: 61) sts.
Complete to match left front, reversing shaping

and working first row of neck shaping as folls:
Next row (RS): Patt 25 (24: 25: 25: 25: 25) sts and slip these sts onto a holder, K to last 0 (3: 3: 3: 3: 3) sts, (K2tog tbl, K1) 0 (1: 1: 1: 1: 1) times.
13 (16: 16: 18: 18: 20) sts.

SLEEVES (both alike)

Cast on 61 (63: 65: 67: 69: 71) sts using 3mm (US 2/3) needles.
Work in rib as given for back for 8 rows, inc 1 st at each end of 5th of these rows and ending with a WS row.
63 (65: 67: 69: 71: 73) sts.
Change to 3¾mm (US 5) needles.
Beg with a K row, work in st st for 2 rows, ending with a WS row.

Shape raglan

Cast off 4 sts at beg of next 2 rows.
55 (57: 59: 61: 63: 65) sts.
Work 2 rows.
Working all raglan decreases in same way as for back and front raglan armhole decreases, dec 1 st at each end of next and 5 (7: 6: 7: 7: 8) foll 4th rows, then on foll 4 (2: 4: 3: 3: 3) alt rows. 35 (37: 37: 39: 41: 41) sts.
Work 1 row, ending with a WS row.

Left sleeve only

Dec 1 st at each end of next row, then cast off 6 (5: 5: 7: 6: 6) sts at beg of foll row.
27 (30: 30: 30: 33: 33) sts.
Dec 1 st at beg of next row, then cast off 6 (7: 7: 7: 8: 8) sts at beg of foll row.
20 (22: 22: 22: 24: 24) sts.

Right sleeve only

Cast off 7 (6: 6: 8: 7: 7) sts at beg and dec 1 st at end of next row.
27 (30: 30: 30: 33: 33) sts.
Work 1 row.
Cast off 6 (7: 7: 7: 8: 8) sts at beg and dec 1 st at end of next row.
20 (22: 22: 22: 24: 24) sts.
Work 1 row.

Both sleeves

Rep last 2 rows twice more.
Cast off rem 6 sts.

MAKING UP

Pin the pieces out and steam gently without allowing the iron to touch the yarn.
Join all 4 raglan seams using back stitch or mattress stitch if preferred.

Neckband

With RS facing and using 3mm (US 2/3) needles, slip 25 (24: 25: 25: 25: 25) sts from right front holder onto right needle, rejoin yarn and pick up and knit 10 (12: 12: 14: 14: 16) sts up right side of neck, 30 (32: 32: 34: 36: 36) sts from top of left sleeve, 51 (51: 53: 55: 55: 57) sts from back, 30 (32: 32: 34: 36: 36) sts from top of right sleeve, and 10 (12: 12: 14: 14: 16) sts down left side of neck, then patt 25 (24: 25: 25: 25: 25) sts from left front holder.
181 (187: 191: 201: 205: 211) sts.
Row 1 (WS): Patt 6 sts, K1, *P1, K1, rep from * to last 6 sts, patt 6 sts.
Row 2 (buttonhole row): K2, K2tog, yfwd (to make 9th buttonhole), K2, P1, *K1, P1, rep from * to last 6 sts, patt 6 sts.
These 2 rows set the sts – front opening edge 6 sts still in ridge patt (for front band) with all other sts now in rib.
Cont as set for a further 2 rows, ending with a **RS** row.
Cast off in patt (on **WS**).
Join side and sleeve seams. Sew on buttons.

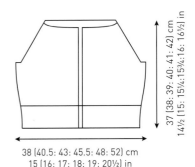

38 (40.5: 43: 45.5: 48: 52) cm
15 (16: 17: 18: 19: 20½) in

37 (38: 39: 40: 41: 42) cm
14½ (15: 15¼: 15¾: 16: 16½) in

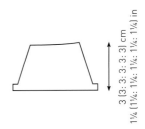

3 (3: 3: 3: 3: 3) cm
1¼ (1¼: 1¼: 1¼: 1¼: 1¼) in

NAT
CABLED A-LINE JACKET

Recommendation
Suitable for the knitter with a little experience
Please see page 23 for photograph.

	XS	S	M	L	XL	XXL	
To fit	**81**	**86**	**91**	**97**	**102**	**109**	**cm**
bust	32	34	36	38	40	43	**in**

Rowan Big Wool
10	10	11	11	12	13	x 100gm

Photographed in Black

Needles
1 pair 10mm (no 000) (US 15) needles
Cable needle

Buttons – 4

Tension
10 sts and 13 rows to 10 cm measured over
textured pattern using 10mm (US 15) needles.

Special abbreviations
cn = cable needle; **C4B** = slip next 2 sts onto
cn and leave at back of work, K2, then K2 from
cn; **C4F** = slip next 2 sts onto cn and leave at
front of work, K2, then K2 from cn; **C6B** = slip
next 3 sts onto cn and leave at back of work,
K3, then K3 from cn; **C6F** = slip next 3 sts
onto cn and leave at front of work, K3, then
K3 from cn; **C8B** = slip next 4 sts onto cn and
leave at back of work, K4, then K4 from cn;
C8F = slip next 4 sts onto cn and leave at front
of work, K4, then K4 from cn.

BACK
Cast on 59 (61: 63: 65: 67: 69) sts using
10mm (US 15) needles.
Row 1 (inc) (RS): P0 (0: 1: 1: 0: 1), (K1 tbl,
P1) 4 (4: 4: 4: 5: 5) times, *(K1, inc in next st,
K1) twice, P1, (K1, inc in next st, K1) twice*,
P1, (K1 tbl, P1) 8 (9: 9: 10: 10: 10) times,
rep from * to * once more, (P1, K1 tbl)
4 (4: 4: 4: 5: 5) times, P0 (0: 1: 1: 0: 1).
67 (69: 71: 73: 75: 77) sts.
Row 2: K8 (8: 9: 9: 10: 11), *P8, K1, P8*,
K17 (19: 19: 21: 21: 21), rep from * to *
once more, K8 (8: 9: 9: 10: 11).
These 2 rows form textured patt between
cables and at sides.
Keeping textured patt correct, cont as folls:
Row 3: Patt 8 (8: 9: 9: 10: 11) sts, *K8, P1,
K8*, patt 17 (19: 19: 21: 21: 21) sts, rep from
* to * once more, patt 8 (8: 9: 9: 10: 11) sts.
Rows 4 to 9: As rows 2 and 3, 3 times.
Row 10: As row 2.
Row 11: Patt 8 (8: 9: 9: 10: 11) sts, *C8B, P1,
C8F*, patt 17 (19: 19: 21: 21: 21) sts,
rep from * to * once more, patt 8 (8: 9: 9:
10: 11) sts.
Rows 12 to 19: As rows 2 and 3, 4 times.
Row 20: As row 2.
Row 21: Patt 8 (8: 9: 9: 10: 11) sts, *slip next
4 sts onto cn and leave at back of work, K2,
K2tog, then K2tog, K2 from cn, P1, slip next
4 sts onto cn and leave at front of work, K2,
K2tog, then K2tog, K2 from cn*, patt 17 (19:
19: 21: 21: 21) sts, rep from * to * once more,
patt 8 (8: 9: 9: 10: 11) sts.
59 (61: 63: 65: 67: 69) sts.
Row 22: Patt 8 (8: 9: 9: 10: 11) sts, *P6, K1,
P6*, patt 17 (19: 19: 21: 21: 21) sts, rep from
* to * once more, patt 8 (8: 9: 9: 10: 11) sts.
Row 23: Patt 8 (8: 9: 9: 10: 11) sts, *K6, P1,
K6*, patt 17 (19: 19: 21: 21: 21) sts, rep from
* to * once more, patt 8 (8: 9: 9: 10: 11) sts.
Rows 24 to 27: As rows 22 and 23, twice.
Row 28: As row 22.
Row 29: Patt 8 (8: 9: 9: 10: 11) sts, *C6B, P1,
C6F*, patt 17 (19: 19: 21: 21: 21) sts, rep from
* to * once more, patt 8 (8: 9: 9: 10: 11) sts.

Rows 30 to 33: As rows 22 and 23, twice.
Row 34: As row 22.
Row 35: As row 29.
Rows 36 to 39: As rows 22 and 23, twice.
Row 40: As row 22.
Row 41: Patt 8 (8: 9: 9: 10: 11) sts, *slip next
3 sts onto cn and leave at back of work, K1,
K2tog, then K2tog, K1 from cn, P1, slip next
3 sts onto cn and leave at front of work, K1,
K2tog, then K2tog, K1 from cn*, patt 17 (19:
19: 21: 21: 21) sts, rep from * to * once more,
patt 8 (8: 9: 9: 10: 11) sts.
51 (53: 55: 57: 59: 61) sts.
Row 42: Patt 8 (8: 9: 9: 10: 11) sts, *P4, K1,
P4*, patt 17 (19: 19: 21: 21: 21) sts, rep from
* to * once more, patt 8 (8: 9: 9: 10: 11) sts.
Row 43: Patt 8 (8: 9: 9: 10: 11) sts, *K4, P1,
K4*, patt 17 (19: 19: 21: 21: 21) sts, rep from
* to * once more, patt 8 (8: 9: 9: 10: 11) sts.
Row 44: As row 42.
Row 45: Patt 8 (8: 9: 9: 10: 11) sts, *C4B, P1,
C4F*, patt 17 (19: 19: 21: 21: 21) sts, rep from
* to * once more, patt 8 (8: 9: 9: 10: 11) sts.
Rows 42 to 45 form patt for rest of back.
Cont in patt for a further 7 (7: 9: 9: 11: 11)
rows, ending with a WS row.
Shape armholes
Keeping patt correct, cast off 2 sts at beg
of next 2 rows.
47 (49: 51: 53: 55: 57) sts.
Dec 1 st at each end of next 3 rows, then
on foll alt row.
39 (41: 43: 45: 47: 49) sts.
Work 17 (19: 19: 21: 21: 23) rows, ending
with a WS row.
Shape shoulders and back neck
Next row (RS): Cast off 7 (7: 7: 7: 8: 8) sts,
patt until there are 8 (8: 9: 9: 9: 10) sts on
right needle and turn, leaving rem sts on
a holder.
Work each side of neck separately.
Cast off 2 sts at beg of next row.
Cast off rem 6 (6: 7: 7: 7: 8) sts.
With RS facing, rejoin yarn to rem sts, cast off
centre 9 (11: 11: 13: 13: 13) sts, patt to end.
Complete to match first side, reversing shapings.

LEFT FRONT

Cast on 34 (35: 36: 37: 38: 39) sts using 10mm (US 15) needles.

Row 1 (inc) (RS): P0 (0: 1: 1: 0: 1), (K1 tbl, P1) 4 (4: 4: 4: 5: 5) times, (K1, inc in next st, K1) twice, P1, (K1, inc in next st, K1) twice, (P1, K1 tbl) 4 (4: 4: 5: 5: 5) times, P0 (1: 1: 0: 0: 0), K5.
38 (39: 40: 41: 42: 43) sts.

Row 2: K13 (14: 14: 15: 15: 15), P8, K1, P8, K8 (8: 9: 9: 10: 11).

These 2 rows set the sts either side of cable – front opening edge 5 sts in garter st (for front band) and all other sts in textured patt.
Keeping textured patt and garter st correct, cont as folls:

Row 3: Patt 8 (8: 9: 9: 10: 11) sts, K8, P1, K8, patt 13 (14: 14: 15: 15: 15) sts.

Rows 4 to 9: As rows 2 and 3, 3 times.

Row 10: As row 2.

Row 11: Patt 8 (8: 9: 9: 10: 11) sts, C8B, P1, C8F, patt 13 (14: 14: 15: 15: 15) sts.

Rows 12 to 19: As rows 2 and 3, 4 times.

Row 20: As row 2.

Row 21: Patt 8 (8: 9: 9: 10: 11) sts, slip next 4 sts onto cn and leave at back of work, K2, K2tog, then K2tog, K2 from cn, P1, slip next 4 sts onto cn and leave at front of work, K2, K2tog, then K2tog, K2 from cn, patt 13 (14: 14: 15: 15: 15) sts.
34 (35: 36: 37: 38: 39) sts.

Row 22: Patt 13 (14: 14: 15: 15: 15) sts, P6, K1, P6, patt 8 (8: 9: 9: 10: 11) sts.

Row 23: Patt 8 (8: 9: 9: 10: 11) sts, K6, P1, K6, patt 13 (14: 14: 15: 15: 15) sts.

Rows 24 to 27: As rows 22 and 23, twice.

Row 28: As row 22.

Row 29: Patt 8 (8: 9: 9: 10: 11) sts, C6B, P1, C6F, patt 13 (14: 14: 15: 15: 15) sts.

Rows 30 to 33: As rows 22 and 23, twice.

Row 34: As row 22.

Row 35: As row 29.

Rows 36 to 39: As rows 22 and 23, twice.

Row 40: As row 22.

Row 41: Patt 8 (8: 9: 9: 10: 11) sts, slip next 3 sts onto cn and leave at back of work, K1, K2tog, then K2tog, K1 from cn, P1, slip next 3 sts onto cn and leave at front of work, K1, K2tog, then K2tog, K1 from cn, patt 13 (14: 14: 15: 15: 15) sts.
30 (31: 32: 33: 34: 35) sts.

Row 42: Patt 13 (14: 14: 15: 15: 15) sts, P4, K1, P4, patt 8 (8: 9: 9: 10: 11) sts.

Row 43: Patt 8 (8: 9: 9: 10: 11) sts, K4, P1, K4, patt 13 (14: 14: 15: 15: 15) sts.

Row 44: As row 42.

Row 45: Patt 8 (8: 9: 9: 10: 11) sts, C4B, P1, C4F, patt 13 (14: 14: 15: 15: 15) sts.
Rows 42 to 45 form patt for rest of left front.
Cont in patt for a further 7 (7: 9: 9: 11: 11) rows, ending with a WS row.

Shape armhole

Keeping patt correct, cast off 2 sts at beg of next row.
28 (29: 30: 31: 32: 33) sts.
Work 1 row.
Dec 1 st at armhole edge of next 3 rows, then on foll alt row.
24 (25: 26: 27: 28: 29) sts.
Work 9 (11: 11: 11: 11: 13) rows, ending with a WS row.

Shape neck

Next row (RS): Patt 17 (17: 18: 19: 20: 21) sts and turn, leaving rem 7 (8: 8: 8: 8: 8) sts on a holder.
Keeping patt correct, dec 1 st at neck edge of next 2 rows, then on foll 2 (2: 2: 3: 3: 3) alt rows. 13 (13: 14: 14: 15: 16) sts.
Work 1 row, ending with a WS row.

Shape shoulder

Cast off 7 (7: 7: 7: 8: 8) sts at beg of next row.
Work 1 row.
Cast off rem 6 (6: 7: 7: 7: 8) sts.

RIGHT FRONT

Cast on 34 (35: 36: 37: 38: 39) sts using 10mm (US 15) needles.

Row 1 (inc) (RS): K5, P0 (1: 1: 0: 0: 0), (K1 tbl, P1) 4 (4: 4: 5: 5: 5) times, (K1, inc in next st, K1) twice, P1, (K1, inc in next st, K1) twice, (P1, K1 tbl) 4 (4: 4: 4: 5: 5) times, P0 (0: 1: 1: 0: 1). 38 (39: 40: 41: 42: 43) sts.

Row 2: K8 (8: 9: 9: 10: 11), P8, K1, P8, K13 (14: 14: 15: 15: 15).

These 2 rows set the sts either side of cable – front opening edge 5 sts in garter st (for front band) and all other sts in textured patt.
Keeping textured patt and garter st correct, cont as folls:

Row 3: Patt 13 (14: 14: 15: 15: 15) sts, K8, P1, K8, patt 8 (8: 9: 9: 10: 11) sts.

Rows 4 to 9: As rows 2 and 3, 3 times.

Row 10: As row 2.

Row 11: Patt 13 (14: 14: 15: 15: 15) sts, C8B, P1, C8F, patt 8 (8: 9: 9: 10: 11) sts.

Rows 12 to 19: As rows 2 and 3, 4 times.

Row 20: As row 2.

Row 21: Patt 13 (14: 14: 15: 15: 15) sts, slip next 4 sts onto cn and leave at back of work, K2, K2tog, then K2tog, K2 from cn, P1, slip next 4 sts onto cn and leave at front of work, K2, K2tog, then K2tog, K2 from cn, patt 8 (8: 9: 9: 10: 11) sts. 34 (35: 36: 37: 38: 39) sts.
Complete to match left front, reversing shapings, making buttonholes in rows 39 (41: 43: 43: 45: 47) and 2 foll 10th rows, and working first row of neck shaping as folls:

Buttonhole row (RS): K2, cast off 2 sts (to make a buttonhole – cast on 2 sts over these cast-off sts on next row), patt to end.

First row of neck shaping (RS): K2, cast off 2 sts (to make 4th buttonhole – cast on 2 sts over these cast-off sts on first row of neckband), patt until 17 (17: 18: 19: 20: 21) sts rem on **left** needle and slip sts on right needle onto a holder, patt to end.

SLEEVES (both alike)

Cuff (knitted sideways)

Cast on 21 sts using 10mm (US 15) needles.
Now work in patt as folls:

Row 1 (RS): K10, P1, K10.

Row 2: K4, P6, K1, P6, K4.

Rows 3 and 4: As rows 1 and 2.

Row 5: K4, C6B, P1, C6F, K4.

Row 6: As row 2.

Rows 7 and 8: As rows 1 and 2.
These 8 rows form patt.
Cont in patt until cuff measures approx 37 (39: 41: 45: 47: 49) cm, ending after patt row 8 and with a WS row.
Cast off but do NOT fasten off.

Main section

With RS facing and using 10mm (US 15) needles, pick up and knit 37 (39: 41: 45: 47: 49) sts evenly along row-end edge next to last cast-off st.
Now work in patt as folls:

Row 1 (WS): Knit.

Row 2: P1, *K1 tbl, P1, rep from * to end.
These 2 rows form patt.
Cont in patt, shaping sides by dec 1 st at each end of 4th and 3 foll 6th rows.
29 (31: 33: 37: 39: 41) sts.
Work 7 (7: 9: 9: 11: 11) rows, ending with a WS row.

Shape top

Keeping patt correct, cast off 2 sts at beg of next 2 rows. 25 (27: 29: 33: 35: 37) sts.

Dec 1 st at each end of next and 1 (2: 2: 2: 2: 2) foll 4th rows, then on foll 2 (2: 2: 3: 3: 4) alt rows, then on foll 3 rows, ending with a WS row.
Cast off rem 11 (11: 13: 15: 17: 17) sts.

MAKING UP
Press all pieces using a warm iron over a damp cloth.
Join both shoulder seams using back stitch or mattress stitch if preferred.

Neckband
With RS facing and using 10mm (US 15) needles, slip sts from right front holder onto right needle, rejoin yarn and pick up and knit 10 (10: 10: 12: 12: 12) sts up right side of neck, 13 (15: 15: 17: 17: 17) sts from back, and 10 (10: 10: 12: 12: 12) sts down left side of neck, then patt 7 (8: 8: 8: 8: 8) sts from left front holder.
Next row (WS): K to end, casting on 2 sts over those cast off for 4th buttonhole.
47 (51: 51: 57: 57: 57) sts.
Work in garter st for 5 rows, ending with a **RS** row.
Cast off knitwise (on **WS**).
Join side seams. Join sleeve seams. Fold 4 sts to inside around lower edge of cuff and neatly slip stitch in place. Insert sleeves into armholes. Sew on buttons.

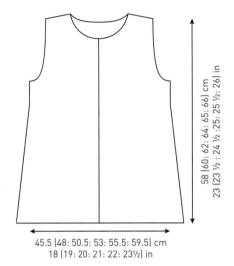

45.5 (48: 50.5: 53: 55.5: 59.5) cm
18 (19: 20: 21: 22: 23½) in

58 (60: 62: 64: 65: 66) cm
23 (23 ½ : 24 ½ :25: 25 ½: 26) in

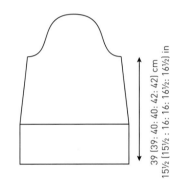

39 (39: 40: 40: 42: 42) cm
15½ (15½ : 16: 16: 16½: 16½) in

BEA

TEXTURED CARDIGAN WITH CORDING DETAIL

Recommendation

Suitable for the knitter with a little experience.
Please see page 29 for photograph.

	XS	S	M	L	X	XXL	
To fit	**81**	**86**	**91**	**97**	**102**	**107**	**cm**
bust	32	34	36	38	40	42	in

Rowan Wool Cotton

10	11	11	12	13	14 x 50gm

Photographed in Clear

Needles

1 pair 3 ¼ mm (no 10) (US 3) needles
1 pair 3 ¾ mm (no 9) (US 5) needles
1 pair 3 ¼ mm (no 10) (US 3) double-pointed
needles

Buttons – 6

Tension

23 sts and 30 rows to 10 cm measured
over textured pattern using 3 ¾ mm (US 5)
needles.

Special abbreviations

Cluster 2 = yrn, P2, lift the yrn over last 2 sts
and off RH needle.
MP = Make picot: cast on 1 st, cast off 1 st.
(See information page for details)

BACK

Cast on 98 (104: 110: 116: 122: 128) sts
using 3 ¼ mm (US 3) needles and work 20
rows in garter st, ending with a WS row.
Mark the 25th (26th: 27th: 28th: 29th: 30th)
st in from each end of last row.
Next row (RS)(dec): K2, K2tog, (K to 3 sts
before marked stitch, K2tog, K3, K2tog tbl)
twice, K to last 4 sts, K2tog tbl, K2.
92 (98: 104: 110: 116: 122) sts.
Work 17 rows in garter st, ending with a WS row.
Rep last 18 rows once, then the first of these
rows (the dec row) once again.
80 (86: 92: 98: 104: 110) sts.
Work 9 rows in garter st, ending with a WS row.
Next row (RS): Knit.
Next row: Purl.
Next row (RS)(eyelet row): K1 (4: 2: 5: 3: 6),
*K2tog, yon, K5 (5: 6: 6: 7: 7), rep from * 4
times more, K2tog, yon, K4, **yon, K2tog tbl,
K5 (5: 6: 6: 7: 7), rep from ** 4 times more,
yon, K2tog tbl, K1 (4: 2: 5: 3: 6).
Next row: Purl.
Change to 3 ¾ mm (US 5) needles and cont
in textured patt as folls:
Row 1 (RS): Knit.
Row 2: P3 (6: 3: 6: 3: 6), *cluster 2, P4, rep
from * to last 5 (8: 5: 8: 5: 8) sts, cluster 2,
P3 (6: 3: 6: 3: 6).
Rows 3 & 5: As row 1.
Row 4: Purl.
Row 6: P6 (3: 6: 3: 6: 3), *cluster 2, P4, rep
from * to last 8 (5: 8: 5: 8: 5) sts, cluster 2,
P6 (3: 6: 3: 6: 3).
Row 7: K2, M1, K to last 2 sts, M1, K2.
82 (88: 94: 100: 106: 112) sts.
Row 8: Purl.
Rows 1 – 8 form the patt and start side seam
shaping.
Cont in patt, inc 1 st at each end of 7th row
and 3 foll 8th rows, then on every foll 6th row
until there are 94 (100: 106: 112: 118: 124)
sts, taking inc sts into patt.
Cont straight until back measures 20 (20: 21:
21: 22: 22) cm from needle change i.e. two
rows above eyelet row, ending with a WS row.

Shape armholes

Keeping patt correct, cast off 4 (4: 5: 5: 6: 7)
sts at beg of next 2 rows.
86 (92: 96: 102: 106: 110) sts.
Dec 1 st at each end of next 5 (7: 7: 9: 9: 11)
rows, then on every foll alt row until 72 (74:
76: 80: 82: 84) sts rem.
Cont straight until armhole measures
18 (19: 19: 20: 20: 21) cm, ending with a
WS row.

Shape shoulders and back neck

Cast off 5 (5: 5: 6: 6: 6) sts at beg of next
2 rows. 62 (64: 66: 68: 70: 72) sts.
Cast off 5 (5: 5: 6: 6: 6) sts at beg of next row,
patt until there are 9 (9: 10: 9: 10: 10) sts on
RH needle and turn, leaving rem sts on a holder.
Work each side of neck separately.
Cast off 4 sts at beg of next row.
Cast off rem 5 (5: 6: 5: 6: 6) sts.
With RS facing, rejoin yarn to sts from holder,
cast off centre 34 (36: 36: 38: 38: 40) sts,
patt to end.
Work to match first side, reversing shapings.

LEFT FRONT

Cast on 59 (62: 65: 68: 71: 74) sts using
3 ¼ mm (US 3) needles and work as folls:
Next row (RS): Knit.
Next row: MP, K to end.
Next row: Knit.
Next row: Knit.
These 4 rows form garter st with picot trim
edging.
Work a further 16 rows as set, ending with
a WS row.
Mark the 25th (26th: 27th: 28th: 29th: 30th)
st in from end of last row.
Next row (RS)(dec): K2, K2tog, K to 3 sts
before marked st, K2tog, K3, K2tog tbl,
K to end.
56 (59: 62: 65: 68: 71) sts.
Work 17 rows, ending with a WS row.
Rep last 18 rows once, then the first of these
rows (the dec row) once again.
50 (53: 56: 59: 62: 65) sts.
Work 9 rows, ending with a WS row.

Next row (RS): Knit.

Next row: Patt 12, P to end.

Next row (RS) (eyelet row): K1 (4: 2: 5: 3: 6), *K2tog, yon, K5 (5: 6: 6: 7: 7), 4 times more, K2tog, yon, K to end.

Next row: Patt 12, P to end.

Change to 3 ¾ mm (US 5) needles and cont in textured patt as folls:

Row 1 (RS): Knit.

Row 2: Patt 12, P3, *cluster 2, P4, rep from * to last 5 (8: 5: 8: 5: 8) sts, cluster 2, P3 (6: 3: 6: 3: 6).

Rows 3 & 5: As row 1.

Row 4: Patt 12, P to end.

Row 6: Patt 12, *cluster 2, P4, rep from * to last 8 (5: 8: 5: 8: 5) sts, cluster 2, P6 (3: 6: 3: 6: 3).

Row 7: K2, M1, K to end.
51 (54: 57: 60: 63: 66) sts.

Row 8: Patt 12, P to end.

Rows 1 – 8 form the patt and start side seam shaping.

Cont in patt, inc 1 st at beg of 7th row and 3 foll 8th rows, then on every foll 6th row until there are 57 (60: 63: 66: 69: 72) sts, taking inc sts into patt.

Cont straight until left front matches back to beg of armhole shaping, ending with a WS row.

Shape armhole

Keeping patt correct, cast off 4 (4: 5: 5: 6: 7) sts at beg of next row.
53 (56: 58: 61: 63: 65) sts.

Work 1 row.

Dec 1 st at armhole edge of next 5 (7: 7: 9: 9: 11) rows, then on every foll alt row until 46 (47: 48: 50: 51: 52) sts rem.

Cont straight until 16 (16: 16: 18: 18: 18) rows less have been worked than on back to start of shoulder shaping, ending with a WS row.

Shape neck

Next row (RS): Patt to last 22 (23: 23: 23: 23: 24) sts and turn, leaving rem sts on a holder for neckband.

Dec 1 st at neck edge on next 6 rows, then on 2 (2: 2: 3: 3: 3) foll alt rows, then on foll 4th row. 15 (15: 16: 17: 18: 18) sts.

Work 1 row.

Shape shoulder

Cast off 5 (5: 5: 6: 6: 6) sts at beg of next and foll alt row.

Work 1 row.

Cast off rem 5 (5: 6: 5: 6: 6) sts.

Mark the positions of 6 buttons on left front, the first two to come 2.5 cm either side of eyelet row, the last one to come 4 rows below start of neck shaping, and rem buttons spaced evenly between.

Working 6 buttonholes to correspond with positions marked for buttons, buttonhole is worked as folls:

Buttonhole row (RS): Patt 5, cast off 3, patt to end and back, casting on 3 sts over those cast-off on previous row.

Work right front as folls:

RIGHT FRONT

Cast on 59 (62: 65: 68: 71: 74) sts using 3 ¼ mm (US 3) needles and work as folls:

Next row (RS): Knit.

Next row: Knit.

Next row: MP, K to end.

Next row: Knit.

These 4 rows form garter st with picot trim edging.

Work a further 16 rows as set, ending with a WS row.

Mark the 25th (26th: 27th: 28th: 29th: 30th) st in from beg (side seam edge) of last row.

Next row (RS)(dec): K to 3 sts before marked st, K2tog, K3, K2tog tbl, K to last 4 sts, K2tog tbl, K2. 56 (59: 62: 65: 68: 71) sts.

Work 17 rows, ending with a WS row.

Rep last 18 rows once, then the first of these rows (the dec row) once again.
50 (53: 56: 59: 62: 65) sts.

Work 9 rows, ending with a WS row.

Next row (RS): Patt to end.

Next row: P to last 12 sts, K to end.

Next row (RS)(eyelet row): Patt 12, *yon, K2tog tbl, K5 (5: 6: 6: 7: 7), rep from * 4 times more, yon, K2tog tbl, K1 (4: 2: 5: 3: 6).

Next row: P to last 12 sts, K to end.

Change to 3 ¾ mm (US 5) needles and cont in textured patt as folls:

Row 1 (RS): Patt to end.

Row 2: P3 (6: 3: 6: 3: 6), *cluster 2, P4, rep from * to last 17 sts, cluster 2, P3, K to end.

Rows 3 & 5: As row 1.

Row 4: P to last 12 sts, K to end.

Row 6: P6 (3: 6: 3: 6: 3), *cluster 2, P4, rep from * to last 14 sts, cluster 2, K to end.

Row 7: Patt to last 2 sts, M1, K2.
51 (54: 57: 60: 63: 66) sts.

Row 8: P to last 12 sts, K to end.

Rows 1 – 8 form the patt and start side seam shaping.

Cont in patt, complete to match left front, reversing all shapings.

Do not break yarn at neck edge, join in a new ball of yarn to complete right front, saving the first ball of yarn to work neckband.

SLEEVES (both alike)

Cuff (knitted from side to side)

Cast on 12 (12: 13: 13: 14: 14) sts using 3 ¼ mm (US 3) needles and work as folls:

Next row (RS): Knit.

Next row: Knit.

Next row: MP, K to end.

Next row: Knit.

These 4 rows form garter st with picot trim edging.

Cont in patt as set until 90 (90: 96: 96: 102: 102) rows have been completed, ending with a WS row.

Cast off, but do not break yarn.

Upper sleeve

With RS facing and using 3 ¾ mm (US 5) needles, pick up and knit 58 (58: 62: 62: 66: 66) sts along straight edge of cuff and P 1 row, ending with a WS row.

Row 1 (RS): Knit.

Row 2: P1 (1: 3: 3: 5: 5), *cluster 2, P4, rep from * to last 3 (3: 5: 5: 7: 7) sts, cluster 2, P1 (1: 3: 3: 5: 5).

Rows 3 & 5: As row 1.

Row 4: Purl.

Row 6: P4 (4: 6: 6: 2: 2), *cluster 2, P4, rep from * to last 6 (6: 8: 8: 4: 4) sts, cluster 2, P4 (4: 6: 6: 2: 2).

Row 7: As row 1.

Row 8: Purl.

Rows 1 – 8 form patt and are repeated throughout.

Cont in patt, inc 1 st at each end of next row, then on every foll 12th (12th: 14th: 12th: 16th: 14th) row to 70 (64: 72: 74: 72: 72) sts, then on every foll – (10th : 12th: 10th: 14th: 12th) row until there are – (72: 74: 76: 78: 80) sts, taking inc sts into patt.

Cont straight until sleeve measures 27 (28: 28.5: 29.5: 30: 31) cm from needle change row, ending with a WS row.

Shape sleeve top

Keeping patt correct, cast off 4 (4: 5: 5: 6: 7) sts at beg of next 2 rows.
62 (64: 64: 66: 66: 66) sts.

Dec 1 st at each end of next 5 rows, then on
2 foll alt rows, then on every foll 4th row until
40 (42: 42: 42: 42: 40) sts rem.
Work 1 row, ending with a WS row.
Dec 1 st at each end of next row and 1 (2: 2:
2: 2: 1) foll alt rows, then on every foll
row until 30 sts rem, ending with a WS row.
Cast off.

MAKING UP
Press as described on information page.
Join both shoulder seams using backstitch
or mattress stitch if preferred.

Neckband
With RS facing and using 3 ¼ mm (US 3)
needles and ball of yarn left with right front,
patt across 22 (23: 23: 23: 23: 24) sts from
right front holder, pick up and knit 20 (20: 20:
22: 22: 22) sts up right front neck, 42 (44:
44: 46: 46: 48) sts from back, 20 (20: 20:
22: 22: 22) sts down left front neck, then patt
across 22 (23: 23: 23: 23: 24) sts from left
front holder.
126 (130: 130: 136: 136: 140) sts.
Work 6 rows in garter st with picot trim
edging, ending with a **RS** row.
Cast off knitwise (on WS).

Cording
Cast on 3 sts using 3 ¼ mm (US 3)
doublepointed needles and knit 1 row.
*Without turning needle, slip sts to opposite
end of needle and, taking yarn quite tightly
around back of work to prevent a ladder from
forming, knit these 3 sts again.
Rep from * until belt measures approx 140 cm.
Join side and sleeve seams.
Set sleeves into armholes using the set-in
method.
Sew on buttons to correspond with
buttonholes.
Thread cording through eyelet row at waist
& tie ends of centre front.

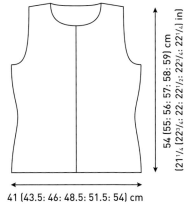

54 (55: 56: 57: 58: 59) cm
(21¼ (22¾: 22: 22½: 22¾: 22¼) in)

41 (43.5: 46: 48.5: 51.5: 54) cm
(16¼ (17¼: 18: 19: 20¼: 21¼) in)

32 (33: 34: 35: 36: 37) cm
(12½ (13: 13½: 13¾: 14¼: 14½) in)

ARCHIE

RAGLAN SWEATER WITH GARTER STITCH YOKE

Recommendation

Suitable for the novice knitter

Please see pages 25-27 for photographs.

	S	M	L	XL	
To fit chest	97	102	107	112	cm
	38	40	42	44	in

Rowan Cashsoft Aran

	14	15	16	17 x 50gm

Photographed in Black

Needles

1 pair 4mm (no 8) (US 6) needles

1 pair 4½mm (no 7) (US 7) needles

4mm (no 8) (US 6) circular needle

Tension

19 sts and 25 rows to 10 cm measured over stocking stitch, 19 sts and 30 rows to 10 cm measured over garter stitch, both using 4½mm (US 7) needles.

BACK

Cast on 101 (105: 111: 115) sts using 4mm (US 6) needles.

Row 1 (RS): K1, *P1, K1, rep from * to end.

Row 2: P1, *K1, P1, rep from * to end.

These 2 rows form rib.

Work in rib for a further 18 rows, ending with a WS row.

Change to 4½mm (US 7) needles.

Beg with a K row, work in st st until back measures 44 cm, ending with a WS row.

Shape raglan armholes

Now working in garter st throughout, cast off 5 sts at beg of next 2 rows.

91 (95: 101: 105) sts.

Work 2 rows.

Next row (RS): K3, K2tog, K to last 5 sts, K2tog tbl, K3. 89 (93: 99: 103) sts.

Working all raglan armhole decreases as set by last row, dec 1 st at each end of 4th and 4 (5: 3: 4) foll 4th rows, then on foll 23 (23: 28: 28) alt rows. 33 (35: 35: 37) sts.

Work 1 row, ending with a WS row.

Cast off.

FRONT

Work as given for back until 47 (49: 51: 53) sts rem in raglan armhole shaping.

Work 1 row, ending with a WS row.

Shape neck

Next row (RS): K3, K2tog, K5 (5: 7: 7) and turn, leaving rem sts on a holder.

Work each side of neck separately.

Dec 1 st at neck edge of next 3 (3: 4: 4) rows **and at same time** dec 1 st at raglan armhole edge of 2nd and foll 0 (0: 1: 1) alt row. 5 sts.

Work 0 (0: 1: 1) row, ending with a WS row.

Next row (RS): K2, K3tog. 3 sts.

Next row: K3.

Next row: sl 1, K2tog, psso.

Next row: P1 and fasten off.

With RS facing, rejoin yarn to rem sts, cast off centre 27 (29: 27: 29) sts, K to last 5 sts, K2tog tbl, K3.

Complete to match first side, reversing shapings.

SLEEVES (both alike)

Cast on 57 (59: 61: 63) sts using 4mm (US 6) needles.

Work in rib as given for back for 18 rows, ending with a WS row.

Change to 4½mm (US 7) needles.

Beg with a K row, work in st st for 2 rows, ending with a WS row.

Next row (inc) (RS): K2, M1, K to last 2 sts, M1, K2. 59 (61: 63: 65) sts.

Working all increases as set by last row, inc 1 st at each end of 12th (12th: 12th: 14th) and every foll 12th (12th: 14th: 14th) row to 67 (67: 77: 79) sts, then on every foll 14th (14th: -: -) row until there are 73 (75: -: -) sts.

Cont straight until sleeve measures 49 (50: 51: 52) cm, ending with a WS row.

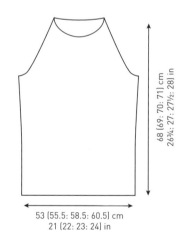

53 (55.5: 58.5: 60.5) cm
21 (22: 23: 24) in

68 (69: 70: 71) cm
26¾: 27: 27½: 28) in

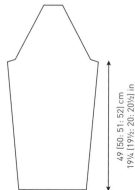

49 (50: 51: 52) cm
19¼ (19½: 20: 20½) in

Continued on next page...

AURA
LACY SCARF & WRAP

Recommendation
Suitable for the knitter with a little experience
Please see pages 28, 29 & 53-55 for photographs.

Rowan Kidsilk Aura
Scarf   6   x 25gm
Photographed in Bark
Wrap   10   x 25gm
Photographed in Nearly Black

Needles
1 pair 8mm (no 0) (US 11) needles

Tension
11½ sts and 12 rows to 10 cm measured over
pattern using 8mm (US 11) needles.

Finished size
Scarf measures 45 cm (17½ in) wide and
250 cm (98½ in) long.
Wrap measures 77 cm (30½ in) wide and
250 cm (98½ in) long.

SCARF and WRAP
Cast on 52 sts for scarf, or 88 sts for wrap,
using 8mm (US 11) needles.
Row 1 (RS): Cast on 2 sts, cast off 2 sts, K
until there are 4 sts on right needle, *K2tog tbl,
(yfwd) twice, K2tog, rep from * to last 4 sts, K4.
Row 2: Cast on 2 sts, cast off 2 sts, K until
there are 4 sts on right needle, *K1, (K1, P1)
into double yfwd of previous row, K1, rep from
* to last 4 sts, K4.
Row 3: Cast on 2 sts, cast off 2 sts, K until
there are 6 sts on right needle, *K2tog tbl,
(yfwd) twice, K2tog, rep from * to last 6 sts, K6.
Row 4: Cast on 2 sts, cast off 2 sts, K until
there are 6 sts on right needle, *K1, (K1, P1)
into double yfwd of previous row, K1, rep from
* to last 6 sts, K6.
These 6 rows form patt.
Cont in patt until work measures 250 cm,
ending with a WS row. Cast off.

Archie – Continued from previous page...

Shape raglan
Now working in garter st throughout, cast off
5 sts at beg of next 2 rows. 63 (65: 67: 69) sts.
Working all raglan decreases in same way as
back raglan armhole decreases, dec 1 st at
each end of 3rd and 9 (10: 11: 12) foll 4th
rows, then on foll 12 (12: 11: 11) alt rows.
19 (19: 21: 21) sts.
Work 1 row, ending with a WS row.
Left sleeve only
Dec 1 st at each end of next row, then cast
off 3 (3: 4: 4) sts at beg of foll row.
14 (14: 15: 15) sts.
Dec 1 st at beg of next row, then cast off 4 sts
at beg of foll row. 9 (9: 10: 10) sts.

Right sleeve only
Cast off 4 (4: 5: 5) sts at beg and dec 1 st at
end of next row. 14 (14: 15: 15) sts.
Work 1 row.
Cast off 4 sts at beg and dec 1 st at end of
next row. 9 (9: 10: 10) sts.
Work 1 row.
Both sleeves
Rep last 2 rows once more.
Cast off rem 4 (4: 5: 5) sts.

MAKING UP
Press all pieces using a warm iron over
a damp cloth. Join all 4 raglan seams using
back stitch or mattress stitch if preferred.

Neckband
With RS facing and using 4mm (US 6)
circular needle, beg and ending at left
back raglan seam, pick up and knit 13 (13:
15: 15) sts from top of left sleeve, 8 (8:
10: 10) sts down left side of neck, 27 (29:
27: 29) sts from front, 8 (8: 10: 10) sts up
right side of neck, 13 (13: 15: 15) sts from
top of right sleeve, then 31 (33: 33: 35) sts
from back.
100 (104: 110: 114) sts.
Round 1 (RS): *K1, P1, rep from * to end.
Rep this round 16 times more.
Cast off in rib.
Join side and sleeve seams.

DUSTY
CABLED A-LINE TUNIC

Recommendation

Suitable for the knitter with a little experience
Please see pages 30-33 for photographs.

	XS	S	M	L	XL	XXL	
To fit	**81**	**86**	**91**	**97**	**102**	**109**	**cm**
bust	32	34	36	38	40	43	in

Rowan Kid Classic

| | 14 | 15 | 16 | 17 | 18 | 19 | x 50gm |

Photographed in Bittersweet

Needles

1 pair 4mm (no 8) (US 6) needles
1 pair 4½mm (no 7) (US 7) needles
Cable needle

Tension

23 sts and 28 rows to 10 cm measured over
textured pattern using 4½mm (US 7) needles.

Special abbreviations

cn = cable needle; **C6B** = slip next 3 sts onto
cn and leave at back of work, K3, then K3 from
cn; **C6F** = slip next 3 sts onto cn and leave at
front of work, K3, then K3 from cn; **C8B** = slip
next 4 sts onto cn and leave at back of work,
K4, then K4 from cn; **C8F** = slip next 4 sts
onto cn and leave at front of work, K4, then K4
from cn; **C10B** = slip next 5 sts onto cn and
leave at back of work, K5, then K5 from cn;
C10F = slip next 5 sts onto cn and leave at
front of work, K5, then K5 from cn.

BACK and FRONT (both alike)

Cast on 149 (155: 161: 167: 173: 183) sts
using 4½mm (US 7) needles.
Row 1 (inc) (RS): P0 (1: 0: 1: 0: 1), (K1 tbl,
P1) 7 (8: 10: 11: 11: 13) times, *(K2, inc in
next st) twice, K2, P1, (K2, inc in next st) twice,
K2, P1, (K1 tbl, P1) 4 (4: 4: 4: 5: 5) times,
rep from * 3 times more, (K2, inc in next st)
twice, K2, P1, (K2, inc in next st) twice, K2,
(P1, K1 tbl) 7 (8: 10: 11: 11: 13) times,
P0 (1: 0: 1: 0: 1).
169 (175: 181: 187: 193: 203) sts.
Now work in patt as folls:
Row 1 (WS): K14 (17: 20: 23: 22: 27),
*P10, K1, P10, K9 (9: 9: 9: 11: 11), rep
from * 3 times more, P10, K1, P10, K14 (17:
20: 23: 22: 27).
Row 2: P0 (1: 0: 1: 0: 1), (K1 tbl, P1) 7 (8: 10:
11: 11: 13) times, *K10, P1, K10, P1, (K1 tbl,
P1) 4 (4: 4: 4: 5: 5) times, rep from * 3 times
more, K10, P1, K10, (P1, K1 tbl) 7 (8: 10: 11:
11: 13) times, P0 (1: 0: 1: 0: 1).
Rows 3 to 6: As rows 1 and 2, twice.
Row 7: As row 1.
Row 8: P0 (1: 0: 1: 0: 1), (K1 tbl, P1) 7 (8: 10:
11: 11: 13) times, *C10B, P1, C10F, P1, (K1
tbl, P1) 4 (4: 4: 4: 5: 5) times, rep from * 3
times more, C10B, P1, C10F, (P1, K1 tbl) 7 (8:
10: 11: 11: 13) times, P0 (1: 0: 1: 0: 1).
Rows 9 to 18: As rows 1 and 2, 5 times.
These 18 rows form patt – 5 pairs of 10 st
cables with textured patt between and at sides.
Cont in patt for a further 43 rows, ending after
patt row 7 and with a WS row.
Next row (dec) (RS): Patt 14 (17: 20: 23: 22:
27) sts, *slip next 5 sts onto cn and leave at
back of work, K3, K2tog, then K2tog, K3 from
cn, P1, slip next 5 sts onto cn and leave at
front of work, K3, K2tog, then K2tog, K3 from
cn, patt 9 (9: 9: 9: 11: 11) sts, rep from * 3
times more, slip next 5 sts onto cn and leave
at back of work, K3, K2tog, then K2tog, K3
from cn, P1, slip next 5 sts onto cn and leave
at front of work, K3, K2tog, then K2tog, K3
from cn, patt 14 (17: 20: 23: 22: 27) sts.
149 (155: 161: 167: 173: 183) sts.

Now working 8 st cables on every foll 14th row
(instead of 10 st cables on every 18th row)
cont in patt as now set for a further 39 rows,
ending 11 rows after a cable row and with
a WS row.
Next row (dec) (RS): Patt 14 (17: 20:
23: 22: 27) sts, *slip next 4 sts onto cn
and leave at back of work, K2, K2tog, then
K2tog, K2 from cn, P1, slip next 4 sts onto
cn and leave at front of work, K2, K2tog,
then K2tog, K2 from cn, patt 9 (9: 9: 9:
11: 11) sts, rep from * 3 times more, slip
next 4 sts onto cn and leave at back of
work, K2, K2tog, then K2tog, K2 from cn,
P1, slip next 4 sts onto cn and leave at
front of work, K2, K2tog, then K2tog, K2
from cn, patt 14 (17: 20: 23: 22: 27) sts.
129 (135: 141: 147: 153: 163) sts.
Now working 6 st cables on every foll 10th row
(instead of 8 st cables on every 14th row) cont
in patt as now set as folls:
Cont straight until work measures 52 (52: 53:
53: 53: 53) cm, ending with a WS row.
Shape armholes
Keeping patt correct, cast off 4 (5: 6: 6: 7: 8)
sts at beg of next 2 rows.
121 (125: 129: 135: 139: 147) sts.
Dec 1 st at each end of next 5 (5: 5: 7: 7: 9)
rows, then on foll 3 (4: 5: 5: 6: 7) alt rows,
then on foll 4th row.
103 (105: 107: 109: 111: 113) sts.
Cont straight until armhole measures
15 (16: 16: 17: 18: 19) cm, ending with
a WS row.
Shape neck
Next row (RS): Patt 17 (18: 19: 20: 19: 20)
sts and turn, leaving rem sts on a holder.
Work each side of neck separately.
Keeping patt correct, dec 1 st at neck edge of
next 3 rows, then on foll 2 alt rows.
12 (13: 14: 15: 14: 15) sts.
Work 2 rows, ending with a WS row.
Shape shoulder
Cast off 4 (4: 4: 5: 4: 5) sts at beg of next and
foll alt row and at same time dec 1 st at neck
edge of next row.

Work 1 row.

Cast off rem 3 (4: 5: 4: 5: 4) sts.

With RS facing, rejoin yarn to rem sts, cast off centre 69 (69: 69: 69: 73: 73) sts decreasing 3 sts at top of each cable, patt to end.

Complete to match first side, reversing shapings.

SLEEVES (both alike)
Cuff (knitted sideways)

Cast on 55 sts using 4½mm (US 7) needles.

Row 1 (RS): K13, P1, K8, P2, K9, P2, K8, P1, K11.

Row 2: K3, P8, K1, P8, K2, P9, K2, P8, K1, P8, K5.

Now work in patt as folls:

Row 1 (RS): K13, P1, K8, P2, K9, P2, K8, P1, K11.

Row 2: K3, P8, K1, P8, K2, P9, K2, P8, K1, P8, K5.

Row 3: K5, C8B, P1, C8F, P2, C6B, K3, P2, C8B, P1, C8F, K3.

Row 4: As row 2.

Rows 5 and 6: As rows 1 and 2.

Row 7: K13, P1, K8, P2, K3, C6F, P2, K8, P1, K11.

Row 8: As row 2.

These 8 rows form patt.

Cont in patt until cuff measures approx 45 (46: 47: 48: 49: 50) cm, ending after patt row 6 and with a WS row.

Cast off but do NOT fasten off.

Main section

With RS facing and using 4½mm (US 7) needles, pick up and knit 95 (97: 99: 101: 103: 105) sts evenly along row-end edge next to last cast-off st.

Now work in patt as folls:

Row 1 (WS): Knit.

Row 2: P1, *K1 tbl, P1, rep from * to end.

These 2 rows form patt.

Cont in patt, shaping sides by dec 1 st at each end of 2nd and 8 foll 4th rows, then on foll 6th row, then on foll 8th row, then on foll 10th row.

71 (73: 75: 77: 79: 81) sts.

Cont straight until sleeve measures 25 (26: 27: 28: 29: 30) cm **from pick-up row**, ending with a WS row.

Shape top

Keeping patt correct, cast off 4 (5: 6: 6: 7: 8) sts at beg of next 2 rows.

63 (63: 63: 65: 65: 65) sts.

Dec 1 st at each end of next 3 rows, then on foll alt row, then on 4 (5: 5: 5: 6: 7) foll 4th rows. 47 (45: 45: 47: 45: 43) sts.

Work 1 row.

Dec 1 st at each end of next and every foll alt row until 37 sts rem, then on foll 3 rows, ending with a WS row. 31 sts.

Cast off 3 sts at beg of next 2 rows.

Cast off rem 25 sts.

MAKING UP

Press all pieces using a warm iron over a damp cloth.

Join both shoulder seams using back stitch or mattress stitch if preferred.

Collar

Cast on 257 (257: 257: 257: 265: 265) sts using 4½mm (US 7) needles.

Now work in patt as folls:

Row 1 (RS): P1, K10, P1, (K1 tbl, P1) 6 times, *K10, P1, K10, P1, (K1 tbl, P1) 4 (4: 4: 4: 5: 5) times*, rep from * to * once more, **K10, P1, K10, P1, (K1 tbl, P1) 6 times, rep from ** once more, rep from * to * twice more, K10, P1, K10, P1, (K1 tbl, P1) 6 times, K10, P1.

Row 2: K1, P10, K13, *P10, K1, P10, K9 (9: 9: 9: 11: 11)*, rep from * to * once more, (P10, K1, P10, K13) twice, rep from * to * twice more, P10, K1, P10, K13, P10, K1.

Rows 3 to 14: As rows 1 and 2, 6 times.

Row 15: P1, C10F, P1, (K1 tbl, P1) 6 times, *C10B, P1, C10F, P1, (K1 tbl, P1) 4 (4: 4: 4: 5: 5) times*, rep from * to * once more, **C10B, P1, C10F, P1, (K1 tbl, P1) 6 times, rep from ** once more, rep from * to * twice more, C10B, P1, C10F, P1, (K1 tbl, P1) 6 times, C10B, P1.

Row 16: As row 2.

Rows 17 to 26: As rows 1 and 2, 5 times.

Row 27 (dec): P1, slip next 5 sts onto cn and leave at front of work, K3, K2tog, then K2tog, K3 from cn, P1, (K1 tbl, P1) 6 times, *slip next 5 sts onto cn and leave at back of work, K3, K2tog, then K2tog, K3 from cn, P1, slip next 5 sts onto cn and leave at front of work, K3, K2tog, then K2tog, K3 from cn, P1, (K1 tbl, P1) 4 (4: 4: 4: 5: 5) times*, rep from * to * once more, **slip next 5 sts onto cn and leave at back of work, K3, K2tog, then K2tog, K3 from cn, P1, slip next 5 sts onto cn and leave at front of work, K3, K2tog, then K2tog, K3 from cn, P1, (K1 tbl, P1) 6 times, rep from ** once more, rep from * to * twice more, slip next 5 sts onto cn and leave at back of work, K3, K2tog, then K2tog, K3 from cn, P1, slip next 5 sts onto cn and leave at front of work, K3, K2tog, then K2tog, K3 from cn, P1, (K1 tbl, P1) 6 times, slip next 5 sts onto cn and leave at back of work, K3, K2tog, then K2tog, K3 from cn, P1.

225 (225: 225: 225: 233: 233) sts.

Now working 8 st cables on every foll 10th row (instead of 10 st cables) cont in patt as now set for a further 19 rows, ending 9 rows after a cable row and with a WS row.

Row 47: P1, slip next 4 sts onto cn and leave at front of work, K2, K2tog, then K2tog, K2 from cn, P1, (K1 tbl, P1) 6 times, *slip next 4 sts onto cn and leave at back of work, K2, K2tog, then K2tog, K2 from cn, P1, slip next 4 sts onto cn and leave at front of work, K2, K2tog, then K2tog, K2 from cn, P1, (K1 tbl, P1) 4 (4: 4: 4: 5: 5) times*, rep from * to * once more, **slip next 4 sts onto cn and leave at back of work, K2, K2tog, then K2tog, K2 from cn, P1, slip next 4 sts onto cn and leave at front of work, K2, K2tog, then K2tog, K2 from cn, P1, (K1 tbl, P1) 6 times, rep from ** once more, rep from * to * twice more, slip next 4 sts onto cn and leave at back of work, K2, K2tog, then K2tog, K2 from cn, P1, slip next 4 sts onto cn and leave at front of work, K2, K2tog, then K2tog, K2 from cn, P1, (K1 tbl, P1) 6 times, slip next 4 sts onto cn and leave at back of work, K2, K2tog, then K2tog, K2 from cn, P1.

193 (193: 193: 193: 201: 201) sts.

Now working 6 st cables on foll 8th row (instead of 8 st cables) cont in patt as now set for a further 8 rows, ending after a cable row and with a RS row.

Row 56 (dec) (WS): K1, (P2tog) 3 times, K13, *(P2tog) 3 times, K1, (P2tog) 3 times, K9 (9: 9: 9: 11: 11)*, rep from * to * once more, **(P2tog) 3 times, K1, (P2tog) 3 times, K13, rep from ** once more, rep from * to * twice more, (P2tog) 3 times, K1, (P2tog) 3 times, K13, (P2tog) 3 times, K1.

145 (145: 145: 145: 153: 153) sts.

Change to 4mm (US 6) needles.

Row 57: P1, K3, P1, (K1, P1) 6 times, *(K3, P1) twice, (K1, P1) 4 (4: 4: 4: 5: 5) times*, rep from * to * once more, **(K3, P1) twice, (K1, P1) 6 times, rep from ** once more, rep from * to * twice more, (K3, P1) twice, (K1, P1) 6 times, K3, P1.

Row 58: K1, P3, K1, (P1, K1) 6 times,
*(P3, K1) twice, (P1, K1) 4 (4: 4: 4: 5: 5)
times*, rep from * to * once more, **(P3, K1)
twice, (P1, K1) 6 times, rep from ** once more,
rep from * to * twice more, (P3, K1) twice,
(P1, K1) 6 times, P3, K1.
Rep last 2 rows 5 times more, ending with
a WS row.
Cast off in patt.
Join row-end edges of collar then, positioning
collar seam level with one shoulder seam, sew
cast-off edge of collar to neck edge. Join side
seams. Join sleeve seams. Fold 5 sts to inside
around lower edge of cuff and neatly slip stitch
in place. Insert sleeves into armholes.

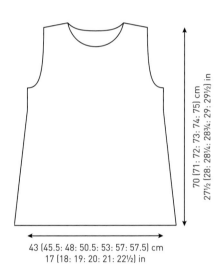

70 (71: 72: 73: 74: 75) cm
27½ (28: 28¼: 28¾: 29: 29½) in

43 (45.5: 48: 50.5: 53: 57: 57.5) cm
17 (18: 19: 20: 21: 22½) in

40 (41: 42: 43: 44: 45) cm
15¾ (16: 16½:17: 17¼: 17¾) in

CHRISTY

DOUBLE FRONTED CARDIGAN WITH GARTER STITCH TRIM

Recommendation

Suitable for the knitter with a little experience
Please see page 35 for photograph.

	XS	S	M	L	XL	XXL	
To fit	**81**	**86**	**91**	**97**	**102**	**107**	cm
bust	32	34	36	38	40	42	in

Rowan Cashsoft 4 ply

	9	9	10	10	11	11 x50gm

Photographed in Sullen

Needles

1 pair 2¾mm (no 12) (US 2) needles
1 pair 3mm (no 11) (US 2/3) needles

Buttons – 4

Tension

28 sts and 38 rows to 10 cm measured over
stocking stitch, using 3mm (US 2/3) needles.

Special abbreviation

MP = Make picot: cast on 1 st, cast off 1 st.
(See information page for details)

BACK

Cast on 120 (128: 136: 142: 150: 158) sts
using 2 ¾mm (US 2) needles.
Work in garter st for 22 (22: 24: 24: 26: 26)
rows, ending with a WS row.
Counting in from both ends of last row, place
markers on 30th (32nd: 34th: 36th: 38th:
40th) sts in from both ends of row.
Next row (dec) (RS): K3, K2tog, (K to within
3 sts of marked st, K2tog, K1, K marked st, K1,
K2tog tbl) twice, K to last 5 sts, K2tog tbl, K3.
Work 21 rows, ending with a WS row.
Rep last 22 rows once more, then first of
these rows (the dec row) again.
102 (110: 118: 124: 132: 140) sts.
Work 9 rows ending with a WS row.
Change to 3mm (US 2/3) needles.
Beg with a K row, cont in st st as folls:
Work 26 rows, ending with a WS row.
Next row (inc) (RS): K3, M1, (K to within
1 st of marked st, M1, K1, K marked st, K1,
M1) twice, K to last 3 sts, M1, K3.
Work 21 rows, ending with a WS row.
Rep last 22 rows once more, then first of
these rows (the inc row) again.
120 (128: 136: 142: 150: 158) sts.
Work a further 9 (9: 13: 13: 17: 17) rows,
ending with a WS row.

Shape raglan armholes

Cast off 5 (5: 6: 6: 7: 7) sts at beg of next 2 rows.
110 (118: 124: 130: 136: 144) sts.
Next row (RS): K1, K2tog, K to last 3 sts,
K2tog, tbl, K1.
Next row: P1, P2tog tbl, P to last 3 sts, P2tog, P1.
Working all raglan armhole decreases as set
by last 2 rows, dec 1 st at each end of next
3 (7: 11: 13: 17: 19) rows, then on foll 30 (30:
28: 29: 27: 29)alt rows, then on foll row,
ending with a WS row.
Cast off rem 38 (38: 40: 40: 42: 42) sts.

LEFT FRONT

Cast on 74 (78: 82: 85: 89: 93) sts using
2 ¾mm (US 2) needles.
Row 1 (RS): Knit.
Row 2: MP, K to end.

Rows 3 and 4: Knit.
These 4 rows form garter st with picot edging.
Working a picot on every 4th row as set throughout,
work in garter st for a further 18 (18: 20: 20:
22: 22) rows, ending with a WS row.
Counting in from end of last row, place marker
on 30th (32nd: 34th: 36th: 38th: 40th) sts in
from end of row.
Next row (dec) (RS): K3, K2tog, K to within
3 sts of marked st, K2tog, K1, K marked st,
K1, K2tog tbl, K to end.
Work 21 rows, ending with a WS row.
Rep last 22 rows once more, then first of
these rows (the dec row) again.
65 (69: 73: 76: 80: 84) sts.
Work 9 rows, ending with a WS row.
Change to 3mm (US 2/3) needles.
Next row (RS): Knit.
Next row: Patt until there are 27 sts on right
needle, P to end.
These 2 rows set the sts – front opening edge
sts still in garter st with picot edging and all
other sts now in st st.
Keeping sts correct as now set, work 1 row,
ending with a RS row.
Next row (short shaping row) (WS): Patt 27,
wrap next st and turn, K to end.
Working this short shaping row after every
6th row (to give the front edge and collar a little
extra length so it sits neatly) and noting that
no further reference will be given to this row
(and it is not included in any row count given),
cont as folls:
Work 11 rows, ending with a WS row.

Shape front slope

Next row (RS): K to last 29 sts, K2tog tbl, K27.
64 (68: 72: 75: 79: 83) sts.
Working all front slope decreases as set by
last row, cont as folls:
Work 11 rows, ending with a WS row.
Next row (inc) (RS): K3, M1, K to within 1 st
of marked st, M1, K1, K marked st, K1, M1, K
to end. 67 (71: 75: 78: 82: 86) sts.
Dec 1 st at front slope edge of 4th (4th: 2nd:
2nd: 2nd: 2nd) and foll 16th (16th: 14th: 16th:
14th: 14th) row. 65 (69: 73: 76: 80: 84) sts.

Work 1 (1: 5: 3: 5: 5) rows, ending with a WS row.

Next row (inc): (RS): K3, M1, K to within 1 st of marked st, M1, K1, K marked st, K1, M1, K to end.

68 (72: 76: 79: 83: 87) sts.

Dec 1 st at front slope edge of 14th (14th: 8th: 12th: 8th: 8th) row.

67 (71: 75: 78: 82: 86) sts.

Work 7 (7: 13: 9: 13: 13) rows, ending with a WS row.

Next row (inc) (RS): K3, M1, K to within 1 st of marked st, M1, K1, K marked st, K1, M1, K to last 0 (0: 0: 0: 29: 29) sts, (K2tog tbl, K27) 0 (0: 0: 0: 1: 1) time.

70 (74: 78: 81: 84: 88) sts.

Dec 1 st at front slope edge of 8th (8th: 2nd: 6th: 14th: 16th) row. 69 (73: 77: 80: 83: 87) sts.

Work 1 (1: 11: 7: 3: 1) rows, ending with a WS row.

Shape raglan armhole

Cast off 5 (5: 6: 6: 7: 7) sts at beg of next row.

64 (68: 71: 74: 76: 80) sts.

Work 1 row.

Working all raglan armhole decreases as set by back, dec 1 st at raglan armhole edge of next 5 (9: 13: 15: 19: 21) rows, then on foll 28 (28: 26: 27: 25: 27) alt rows **and at the same time** dec 1 st at front slope edge of 13th (13th: 3rd: 7th: 9th: 13th) and 0 (0: 0: 0: 1: 0) foll 14th row, then on 2 (0: 3: 3: 2: 3) foll 16th rows, then on 0 (2: 0: 0: 0: 0) foll 18th rows. 28 sts.

Work 1 row, ending with a WS row.

Place marker at end of last row – this will match to top of front raglan edge of sleeve.

Cont as set on these 28 sts only for back neck collar extension for a further 7 (7: 7.5: 7.5: 8: 8) cm, ending with a WS row.

Next row (WS): Patt 6, wrap next st and turn.

Next row: Knit.

Next row: Patt 12, wrap next st and turn.

Next row: Knit.

Next row: Patt 20, wrap next st and turn.

Next row: Knit.

Cast off all 28 sts.

RIGHT FRONT

Cast on 74 (78: 82: 85: 89: 93) sts using 2 ¾mm (US 2) needles.

Rows 1 and 2: Knit.

Row 3 (RS): MP, K to end.

Row 4: Knit.

These 4 rows form garter st with picot edging.

Working a picot on every 4th row as set throughout, work in garter st for a further 18 (18: 20: 20: 22: 22) rows, ending with a WS row.

Counting in from beg of last row, place marker on 30th (32nd: 34th: 36th: 38th: 40th) sts in from beg of row.

Next row (dec) (RS): Patt to within 3 sts of marked st, K2tog, K1, K marked st, K1, K2tog tbl, K to last 5 sts, K2tog tbl, K3.

Work 21 rows ending with a WS row.

Next row (dec) (RS): Patt to within 3 sts of marked st, K2tog, K1, K marked st, K1, K2tog tbl, K to last 5 sts, K2tog tbl, K3.

Work 19 rows, ending with a WS row.

Next row (buttonhole row) (RS): Patt 6, cast off 3 sts (to make first buttonhole of first pair – cast on 3 sts over these cast-off st on next row), K until there are 10 sts on right needle after cast-off, cast off 3 sts (to make 2nd buttonhole of first pair – cast on 3 sts over these cast-off sts on next row), K to end.

Work 1 row.

Next row (dec) (RS): Patt to within 3 sts of marked st, K2tog, K1, K marked st, K1, K2tog tbl, K to last 5 sts, K2tog tbl, K3.

65 (69: 73: 76: 80: 84) sts

Work 9 rows, ending with a WS row.

Change to 3mm (US 2/3) needles.

Next row (RS): Patt to end.

Next row: P to last 27 sts, K to end.

These 2 rows set the sts – front opening edge sts still in garter st with picot edging and all other sts now in st st.

Keeping sts correct as now set, work 2 rows, ending with a WS row.

Next row (short shaping row) (RS): Patt 27, wrap next st and turn, K to end.

Working this short shaping row after every 6th row (to give the front edge and collar a little extra length so it sits neatly) and noting that no further reference will be given to this row (and it is not included in any row count given), cont as folls:

Work 4 rows, ending with a WS row.

Next row (buttonhole row) (RS): Patt 6, cast off 3 sts (to make first buttonhole of 2nd pair – cast on 3 sts over these cast-off sts on next row) K until there are 10 sts on right needle after cast-off, cast off 3 sts (to make 2nd buttonhole of 2nd pair – cast on 3 sts over these cast-off sts on next row), K to end.

Work 3 rows, ending with a WS row.

Shape front slope

Next row (RS): Patt 27, K2tog, K to end.

64 (68: 72: 75: 79: 83) sts.

Working all front shope decreases as set by last row, complete to match left front, rev shapings.

SLEEVES (work both the same)
Cuff

Cast on 17 (17: 18: 18: 19: 19) sts using 2 ¾mm (US 2) needles and work in garter st as folls:

Rows 1 and 2: Knit.

Row 3 (RS): MP, K to end.

Row 4: Knit.

These 4 rows form patt.

Rep last 4 rows a further 38 (39: 40: 41: 42: 43) times, then rows 1 and 2 again, ending with a WS row.

Cast off, but do not break yarn.

Main section

With RS facing and using 3mm (US 2/3) needles, pick up and knit 80 (82: 84: 86: 88: 90) sts along straight edge of cuff and cont as folls:

Next row (WS): Knit.

Beg with a K row, cont in st st as folls:

Next row (dec) (RS): K3, K2tog, K to last 5 sts, K2tog tbl, K3.

Working all decreases as set by last row, dec 1 st at each end of 4th and 4 foll 4th rows.

68 (70: 72: 74: 76: 78) sts.

Work 15 rows, ending with a WS row.

Next row (inc) (RS): K3, M1, K to last 3 sts, M1, K3.

Working all increases as set by last row, inc 1 st at each end of 10th (10th: 10th: 10th: 10th: 12th) and every foll 10th (10th: 10th: 10th: 10th: 12th) row to 82 (84: 82: 80: 94: 94) sts, then on every foll 12th (12th: 12th: 12th: -: 14th) row until there are 86 (88: 90: 92: -: 96) sts.

Cont straight until sleeve measures 37 (37: 38: 39: 40: 41) cm **from pick-up row**, ending with a WS row.

Shape raglan

Cast off 5 (5: 6: 6: 7: 7) sts at beg of next 2 rows. 76 (78: 78: 80: 80: 82) sts.

Working all decreases as set by back raglan decreases, dec 1 st at each end of next 3 (1: 1: 1: 1: 1) rows, then on 0 (0: 0: 1: 1: 3) foll 4th rows, then on every foll alt row until 12 sts rem.

Work 1 row, ending with a WS row.

Left sleeve only

Dec 1 st at each end of next row, then cast off
2 sts at beg of foll row. 8 sts.

Dec 1 st at beg of next row, then cast off 3 sts
at beg of foll row.

Right sleeve only

Cast off 3 sts at beg and dec 1 sat at end
of next row. 8 sts.

Work 1 row.

Rep last 2 rows once more.

Both sleeves

Cast off rem 4 sts.

MAKING UP

Press as described on the information page.
Join raglan seams using backstitch, or
mattress stitch if preferred. With RS together,
join cast-off ends of collar extensions, then
neatly sew in place to top of sleeves and
back neck edge. Sew side and sleeve seams.
Sew on buttons to correspond with
Buttonholes.

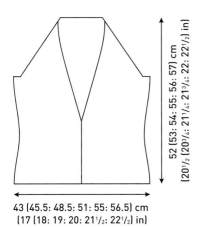

52 (53: 54: 55: 56: 57) cm
(20¹/₂ (20³/₄: 21¹/₄: 21³/₄: 22: 22¹/₂) in)

43 (45.5: 48.5: 51: 55: 56.5) cm
(17 (18: 19: 20: 21¹/₂: 22¹/₂) in)

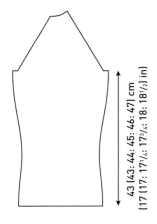

43 (43: 44: 45: 46: 47) cm
(17 (17: 17¹/₄: 17³/₄: 18: 18¹/₂) in)

AAREN
CABLED MINI DRESS

Recommendation

Suitable for the knitter with some experience
Please see pages 36 & 37 for photographs.

	XS	S	M	L	XL	XXL	
To fit	**81**	**86**	**91**	**97**	**102**	**109**	**cm**
bust	32	34	36	38	40	43	**in**

Rowan Cashsoft Aran

	18	19	20	21	22	23 x50gm

Photographed in Thunder

Needles

1 pair 4½mm (no 7) (US 7) needles
1 pair 5mm (no 6) (US 8) needles
Cable needle

Tension

17 sts and 24 rows to 10 cm measured over
stocking stitch using 5mm (US 8) needles.

Special abbreviations

cn = cable needle; **C4B** = slip next 2 sts onto
cn and leave at back of work, K2, then K2 from
cn; **C4F** = slip next 2 sts onto cn and leave at
front of work, K2, then K2 from cn; **Cr3R** = slip
next st onto cn and leave at back of work, K2,
then P1 from cn; **Cr3L** = slip next 2 sts onto
cn and leave at front of work, P1, then K2 from
cn; **C5B** = slip next 3 sts onto cn and leave at
back of work, K2, slip centre st of this group of
5 sts back onto left needle and K this st, then
K2 from cn; **C5F** = slip next 3 sts onto cn and
leave at front of work, K2, slip centre st of this
group of 5 sts back onto left needle and K this
st, then K2 from cn.

BACK

Cast on 106 (110: 114: 118: 122: 130) sts
using 4½mm (US 7) needles.
Beg and ending rows as indicated and foll
chart for body in appropriate size, work chart
rows 1 to 18, ending with a WS row.
Change to 5mm (US 8) needles.
Now repeating the 16, 18 and 20 row patt
reps as on chart, cont from chart as folls:
Work 16 rows, ending with a WS row.
Keeping patt correct, dec 1 st at each
end of next and foll 8th row, then on
6 foll 6th rows.
90 (94: 98: 102: 106: 114) sts.
Work 17 rows, ending with a WS row.
Inc 1 st at each end of next and 2 foll 8th
rows, then on 3 foll 6th rows, taking inc sts
into patt.
102 (106: 110: 114: 118: 126) sts.
Cont straight until back measures 57 (57: 58:
58: 58: 58) cm, ending with a WS row.

Shape armholes

Keeping patt correct, cast off 3 (4: 4: 5: 5: 6)
sts at beg of next 2 rows.
96 (98: 102: 104: 108: 114) sts.
Dec 1 st at each end of next 3 (3: 5: 5: 7: 7)
rows, then on foll 3 (3: 2: 2: 1: 3) alt rows,
then on foll 4th row.
82 (84: 86: 88: 90: 92) sts.
Cont straight until armhole measures 18 (19:
19: 20: 21: 22) cm, ending with a WS row.

Shape shoulders and back neck

Cast off 8 (8: 8: 8: 8: 9) sts at beg of next
2 rows.
66 (68: 70: 72: 74: 74) sts.
Next row (RS): Cast off 8 (8: 8: 8: 8: 9) sts,
patt until there are 11 (11: 12: 12: 13: 12) sts
on right needle and turn, leaving rem sts on a
holder.
Work each side of neck separately.
Cast off 4 sts at beg of next row.
Cast off rem 7 (7: 8: 8: 9: 8) sts.
With RS facing, rejoin yarn to rem sts, cast off
centre 28 (30: 30: 32: 32: 32) sts, patt to end.
Complete to match first side, reversing
shapings.

FRONT

Work as given for back until 22 (22: 22: 24:
24: 24) rows less have been worked than on
back to beg of shoulder shaping, ending with
a WS row.

Shape neck

Next row (RS): Patt 32 (32: 33: 34: 35: 36)
sts and turn, leaving rem sts on a holder.
Work each side of neck separately.
Keeping patt correct, dec 1 st at neck edge
of next 4 rows, then on foll 3 (3: 3: 4: 4: 4) alt
rows, then on 2 foll 4th rows.
23 (23: 24: 24: 25: 26) sts.
Work 3 rows, ending with a WS row.

Shape shoulder

Cast off 8 (8: 8: 8: 8: 9) sts at beg of next
and foll alt row.
Work 1 row.
Cast off rem 7 (7: 8: 8: 9: 8) sts.
With RS facing, rejoin yarn to rem sts, cast off
centre 18 (20: 20: 20: 20: 20) sts, patt to end.
Complete to match first side, reversing shapings.

SLEEVES (both alike)

Cast on 42 (44: 46: 48: 50: 52) sts using
4½mm (US 7) needles.
Row 1 (RS): K0 (1: 0: 0: 0: 1), P2 (2: 0: 1: 2:
2), (K2, P2) 2 (2: 3: 3: 3: 3) times, K4, P1, K2,
P2, K4, P2, K2, P1, K4, (P2, K2) 2 (2: 3: 3: 3:
3) times, P2 (2: 0: 1: 2: 2), K0 (1: 0: 0: 0: 1).
Row 2: P0 (1: 0: 0: 0: 1), K2 (2: 0: 1: 2: 2),
(P2, K2) 2 (2: 3: 3: 3: 3) times, P4, K1, P2, K2,
P4, K2, P2, K1, P4, (K2, P2) 2 (2: 3: 3: 3: 3)
times, K2 (2: 0: 1: 2: 2), P0 (1: 0: 0: 0: 1).
Rows 3 to 6: As rows 1 and 2, twice.

Left sleeve only

Row 7: K0 (1: 0: 0: 0: 1), P2 (2: 0: 1: 2: 2),
(K2, P2) 2 (2: 3: 3: 3: 3) times, C4B, P1, K2,
P2, C4F, P2, K2, P1, C4F, (P2, K2) 2 (2: 3: 3: 3:
3) times, P2 (2: 0: 1: 2: 2), K0 (1: 0: 0: 0: 1).

Right sleeve only

Row 7: K0 (1: 0: 0: 0: 1), P2 (2: 0: 1: 2: 2),
(K2, P2) 2 (2: 3: 3: 3: 3) times, C4B, P1,
K2, P2, C4B, P2, K2, P1, C4F, (P2, K2) 2 (2:
3: 3: 3: 3) times, P2 (2: 0: 1: 2: 2), K0 (1:
0: 0: 0: 1).

XS, S & M BODY CHART

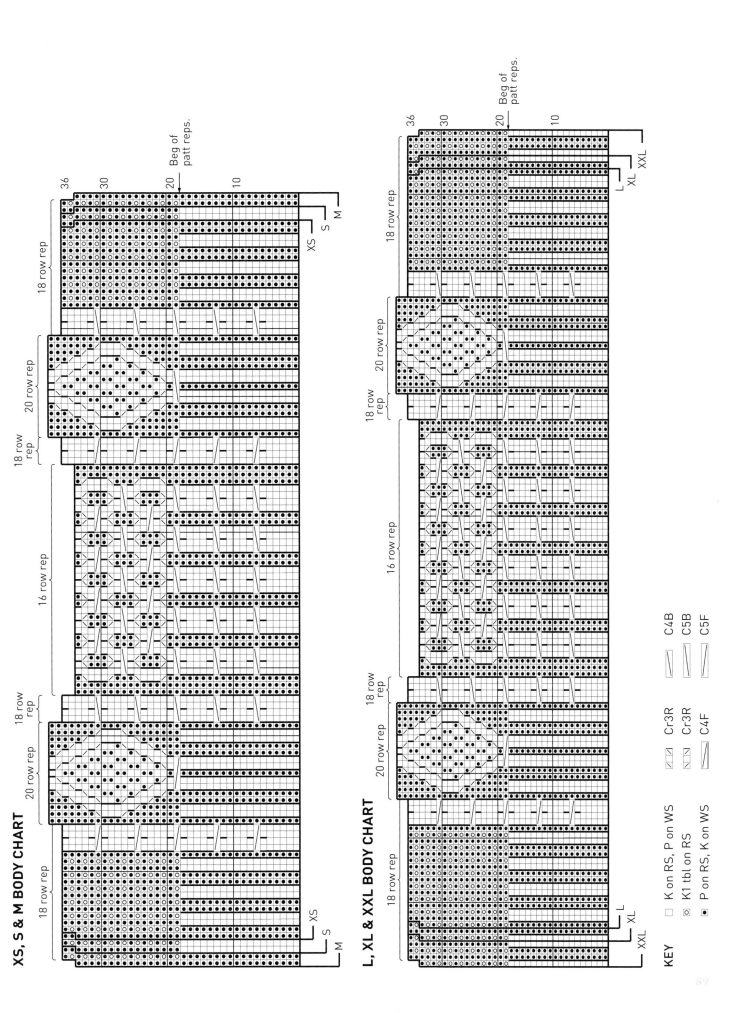

L, XL & XXL BODY CHART

KEY

☐ K on RS, P on WS

◉ K1 tbl on RS

● P on RS, K on WS

▨ Cr3R ╱ C4B

◥ Cr3R ╲ C5B

╱ C4F ╱ C5F

Both sleeves

Row 8: As row 2.

Rows 9 to 12: As rows 1 and 2, twice.

Row 13: As row 7.

Row 14: As row 2.

Rows 15 to 18: As rows 1 and 2 twice, inc 1 st at centre of last row.

43 (45: 47: 49: 51: 53) sts.

Change to 5mm (US 8) needles.

Beg and ending rows as indicated, foll chart for appropriate sleeve and repeating the 18 and 20 row patt reps throughout, cont from chart as folls:

Inc 1 st at each end of next and every foll 10th (8th: 10th: 8th: 10th: 8th) row to 61 (55: 59: 53: 71: 63) sts, then on every foll - (10th: 12th: 10th: -: 10th) row until there are - (65: 65: 69: -: 75) sts, taking inc sts into patt.

Cont straight until sleeve measures 46 (47: 48: 49: 50: 51) cm, ending with a WS row.

Shape top

Keeping patt correct, cast off 3 (4: 4: 5: 5: 6) sts at beg of next 2 rows.

55 (57: 57: 59: 61: 63) sts.

Dec 1 st at each end of next 3 rows, then on foll alt row, then on 4 foll 4th rows.

39 (41: 41: 43: 45: 47) sts.

Work 1 row.

Dec 1 st at each end of next and every foll alt row until 33 sts rem, then on foll 3 rows, ending with a WS row.

Cast off rem 27 sts.

MAKING UP

Press all pieces using a warm iron over a damp cloth.

Join right shoulder seam using back stitch or mattress stitch if preferred.

Neckband

With RS facing and using 4½mm (US 7) needles, pick up and knit 22 (22: 22: 23: 25: 25) sts down left side of neck, 14 (16: 16: 16: 16: 16) sts from front, 21 (21: 21: 22: 24: 24) sts up right side of neck, then 29 (31: 31: 33: 33: 33) sts from back.

86 (90: 90: 94: 98: 98) sts.

Row 1 (WS): P1, *K2, P2, rep from * to last st, K1.

Rep last row 6 times more, ending with a WS row.

Cast off in rib.

Join left shoulder and neckband seam.

Join side seams.

Join sleeve seams.

Insert sleeves into armholes.

RIGHT SLEEVE

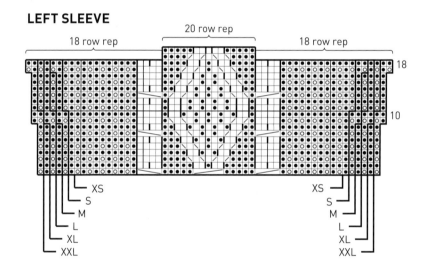

LEFT SLEEVE

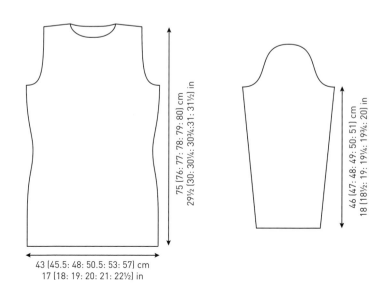

Recommendation

Suitable for the knitter with a little experience
Please see pages 17, 36, 37 & 52 for photographs.

One size

Rowan Kid Classic

2   x 50gm

Photographed in Precious & Smudge

Needles

1 pair 3¾mm (no 9) (US 5) needles
1 pair 4½mm (no 7) (US 7) needles
Cable needle

Tension

23 sts and 28 rows to 10 cm measured over
pattern using 4½mm (US 7) needles.

KAT

CABLED TEXTURED HAT

HAT

Cast on 120 sts using 3¾mm (US 5) needles.
Row 1 (RS): P1, K2, *P2, K2, rep from * to
last st, P1.
Row 2: K1, P2, *K2, P2, rep from * to last st, K1.
These 2 rows form rib.
Work in rib for a further 13 rows, ending with
a **RS** row.
Row 16 (inc) (WS): Rib 3, (M1, rib 1) 4 times,
*rib 5, M1, rib 6, M1, (rib 1, M1) 3 times, rib 2,
work 2 tog, rib 2, (M1, rib 1) 4 times, rep from
* 3 times more, rib 5, M1, rib 6, (M1, rib 1)
4 times, rib 2.
161 sts.
Change to 4½mm (US 7) needles.
Cont in patt as folls:
Row 1 (RS): P1, *K10, (P1, K1 tbl) 5 times,
P1, K10, P1, rep from * to end.
Row 2: K1, *P10, K11, P10, K1, rep from * to end.
Rows 3 to 6: As rows 1 and 2, twice.
Row 7: P1, *slip next 5 sts onto cable needle
and leave at front of work, K5, then K5 from
cable needle, (P1, K1 tbl) 5 times, P1, slip
next 5 sts onto cable needle and leave at
back of work, K5, then K5 from cable needle,
P1, rep from * to end.
Row 8: As row 2.
Rows 9 to 22: As rows 1 and 2, 7 times.
Row 23: As row 7.
Row 24: As row 2.
Rows 25 to 36: As rows 1 and 2, 6 times.
Row 37: P1, *slip next 5 sts onto cable
needle and leave at front of work, K3, K2tog,
then K2tog, K3 from cable needle, (P1, K1
tbl) twice, P3tog, (K1 tbl, P1) twice, slip next
5 sts onto cable needle and leave at back of
work, K3, K2tog, then K2tog, K3 from cable
needle, P1, rep from * to end.
131 sts.
Row 38: K1, *P8, K9, P8, K1, rep from * to end.
Row 39: P1, *K8, (P1, K1 tbl) 4 times, P1, K8,
P1, rep from * to end.

Rows 40 to 45: As rows 38 and 39, 3 times.
Row 46: As row 38.
Row 47: P1, *slip next 4 sts onto cable
needle and leave at front of work, K2, K2tog,
then K2tog, K2 from cable needle, P1, K1 tbl,
P1, K3tog, P1, K1 tbl, P1, slip next 4 sts onto
cable needle and leave at back of work, K2,
K2tog, then K2tog, K2 from cable needle, P1,
rep from * to end.
101 sts.
Row 48: K1, *P6, K7, P6, K1, rep from * to end.
Row 49: P1, *K6, (P1, K1 tbl) 3 times, P1, K6,
P1, rep from * to end.
Rows 50 and 51: As rows 48 and 49.
Row 52: As row 48.
Row 53: P1, *slip next 3 sts onto cable
needle and leave at front of work, K1, K2tog,
then K2tog, K1 from cable needle, P1, K1 tbl,
P3tog, K1 tbl, P1, slip next 3 sts onto cable
needle and leave at back of work, K1, K2tog,
then K2tog, K1 from cable needle, P1, rep
from * to end.
71 sts.
Row 54: K1, *P4, K5, P4, K1, rep from * to end.
Row 55: P1, *K4, (P1, K1 tbl) twice, P1, K4,
P1, rep from * to end.
Row 56: As row 54.
Row 57: P1, *slip next 2 sts onto cable
needle and leave at front of work, K2tog, then
K2tog from cable needle, P1, K3tog, P1, slip
next 2 sts onto cable needle and leave at back
of work, K2tog, then K2tog from cable needle,
P1, rep from * to end. 41 sts.
Row 58: K1, *P2, K3, P2, K1, rep from * to end.
Row 59: P1, *K2tog tbl, P3tog, K2tog, P1, rep
from * to end.
Break yarn and thread through rem 21 sts.
Pull up tight and fasten off securely.

MAKING UP

Join back seam, preferably using mattress
stitch.

ED
CLASSIC CABLED SWEATER

Recommendation

Suitable for the knitter with a little experience
Please see pages 39 & 41 for photographs.

	S	M	L	XL	
To fit chest	**97**	**102**	**107**	**112**	**cm**
	38	40	42	44	in

Rowan Pima Cotton DK

	14	15	16	17 x 50gm

Photographed in Peppercorn

Needles

1 pair 3mm (no 11) (US 2/3) needles
1 pair 3¼mm (no 10) (US 3) needles
Cable needle

Tension

26 sts and 34 rows to 10 cm measured over
stocking stitch using 3¼mm (US 3) needles.

BACK

Cast on 140 (146: 152: 160) sts using 3mm
(US 2/3) needles.
Row 1 (RS): P0 (0: 1: 1), K1 (0: 2: 2), (P2, K2)
4 (5: 5: 6) times, *K2, P1, K10, P1, K4, (P2,
K2) 3 times, rep from * twice more, K2, P1,
K10, P1, K2, (K2, P2) 4 (5: 5: 6) times, K1 (0:
2: 2), P0 (0: 1: 1).
Row 2: K0 (0: 1: 1), P1 (0: 2: 2), (K2, P2) 4 (5:
5: 6) times, *K3, P4, K2, P4, K3, P2, (K2, P2) 3
times, rep from * twice more, K3, P4, K2, P4,
K3, (P2, K2) 4 (5: 5: 6) times, P1 (0: 2: 2), K0
(0: 1: 1).
These 2 rows form rib.
Work in rib for a further 22 rows, ending with
a WS row.
Change to 3¼mm (US 3) needles.
Now work in cable patt as folls:
Row 1 (RS): K17 (20: 23: 27), *K2, P1, K10,
P1, K16, rep from * twice more, K2, P1, K10,
P1, K19 (22: 25: 29).
Row 2: P17 (20: 23: 27), *K3, P4, K2, P4, K3,
P14, rep from * twice more, K3, P4, K2, P4, K3,
P17 (20: 23: 27).
Row 3: K17 (20: 23: 27), *K2, P1, slip next 6
sts onto cn and leave at back of work, K4, slip
centre 2 sts of this group of 10 sts back onto
left needle and K these 2 sts, then K4 from cn,
P1, K16, rep from * once more, K2, P1, slip
next 6 sts onto cn and leave at front of work,
K4, slip centre 2 sts of this group of 10 sts
back onto left needle and K these 2 sts, then
K4 from cn, P1, K18, P1, slip next 6 sts onto
cn and leave at front of work, K4, slip
centre 2 sts of this group of 10 sts back onto
left needle and K these 2 sts, then K4 from cn,
P1, K19 (22: 25: 29).
Row 4: As row 2.
Rows 5 to 16: As rows 1 and 2, 6 times.
These 16 rows form patt.
Cont in patt until back measures 46 cm, ending with a WS row.
Shape armholes
Keeping patt correct, cast off 5 sts at beg of
next 2 rows.
130 (136: 142: 150) sts.

Dec 1 st at each end of next 5 (5: 7: 7) rows,
then on foll 4 (4: 4: 5) alt rows, then on foll
4th row.
110 (116: 118: 124) sts.
Cont straight until armhole measures 22 (23:
24: 25) cm, ending with a WS row.
Shape shoulders and back neck
Cast off 9 (10: 10: 10) sts at beg of next
2 rows.
92 (96: 98: 104) sts.
Next row (RS): Cast off 9 (10: 10: 10) sts,
patt until there are 13 (13: 13: 14) sts on right
needle and turn, leaving rem sts on a holder.
Work each side of neck separately.
Cast off 4 sts at beg of next row.
Cast off rem 9 (9: 9: 10) sts.
With RS facing, rejoin yarn to rem sts, cast
off centre 48 (50: 52: 56) sts, patt to end.
Complete to match first side, reversing
shapings.

FRONT

Work as given for back until 20 (20: 22: 22)
rows less have been worked than on back to
beg of shoulder shaping, ending with a WS row.
Shape neck
Next row (RS): Patt 40 (42: 43: 44) sts and
turn, leaving rem sts on a holder.
Work each side of neck separately.
Keeping patt correct, cast off 3 sts at beg
of next row.
37 (39: 40: 41) sts.
Dec 1 st at neck edge of next 5 rows, then
on foll 4 (4: 5: 5) alt rows, then on foll
4th row.
27 (29: 29: 30) sts.
Work 1 row, ending with a WS row.
Shape shoulder
Cast off 9 (10: 10: 10) sts at beg of next
and foll alt row.
Work 1 row.
Cast off rem 9 (9: 9: 10) sts.
With RS facing, rejoin yarn to rem sts, cast
off centre 30 (32: 32: 36) sts, patt to end.
Complete to match first side, reversing
shapings.

SLEEVES (both alike)

Cast on 72 (74: 76: 78) sts using 3mm (US 2/3) needles.

Row 1 (RS): K0 (0: 1: 0), P1 (2: 2: 0), *K2, P2, rep from * to last 3 (0: 1: 2) sts, K2 (0: 1: 2), P1 (0: 0: 0).

Row 2: P0 (0: 1: 0), K1 (2: 2: 0), *P2, K2, rep from * to last 3 (0: 1: 2) sts, P2 (0: 1: 2), K1 (0: 0: 0).

These 2 rows form rib.

Work in rib for a further 18 rows, ending with a WS row.

Inc 1 st at each end of next row.

74 (76: 78: 80) sts.

Work 3 rows, ending with a WS row.

Change to 3¼mm (US 3) needles.

Beg with a K row, work in st st for 8 (8: 10: 10) rows, ending with a WS row.

Next row (inc) (RS): K2, M1, K to last 2 sts, M1, K2.

76 (78: 80: 82) sts.

Working all increases as set by last row, inc 1 st at each end of 12th (12th: 14th: 14th) and every foll 12th (14th: 14th: 14th) row to 80 (96: 98: 96) sts, then on every foll 14th (-: -: 16th) row until there are 94 (-: -: 100) sts.

Cont straight until sleeve measures 50 (51: 52: 53) cm, ending with a WS row.

Shape top

Cast off 5 sts at beg of next 2 rows.

84 (86: 88: 90) sts.

Dec 1 st at each end of next 3 rows, then on foll alt row, then on 8 foll 4th rows.

60 (62: 64: 66) sts.

Work 1 row.

Dec 1 st at each end of next and every foll alt row until 52 sts rem, then on foll 5 rows, ending with a WS row.

Cast off rem 42 sts.

MAKING UP

Press all pieces using a warm iron over a damp cloth.

Join right shoulder seam using back stitch or mattress stitch if preferred.

Neckband

With RS facing and using 3mm (US 2/3) needles, pick up and knit 20 (20: 21: 21) sts down left side of neck, 30 (32: 32: 36) sts from front, 20 (20: 21: 21) sts up right side of neck, then 52 (54: 56: 60) sts from back. 122 (126: 130: 138) sts.

Row 1 (WS): P1, *K2, P2, rep from * to last st, K1.

Rep last row 8 times more, ending with a WS row.

Cast off in rib.

Join left shoulder and neckband seam. Join side seams. Join sleeve seams. Insert sleeves into armholes.

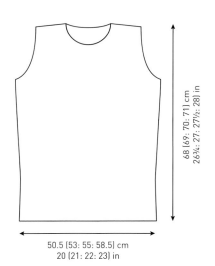

50.5 (53: 55: 58.5) cm
20 (21: 22: 23) in

68 (69: 70: 71) cm
26¾: 27: 27½: 28] in

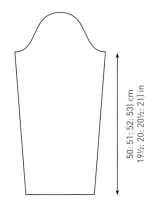

50: 51: 52: 53] cm
19½: 20: 20½: 21] in

RONNIE
TUNIC WITH CABLED TRIMS

Recommendation

Suitable for the knitter with some experience
Please see pages 6-9 for photographs.

	XS	S	M	L	XL	XXL	
To fit	81	86	91	97	102	109	cm
bust	32	34	36	38	40	43	in

Rowan Big Wool

	10	10	11	12	12	13 x 100gm

Photographed in Smoke

Needles

1 pair 10mm (no 000) (US 15) needles
1 pair 12mm (US 17) needles
Cable needle

Tension

8 sts and 13 rows to 10 cm measured over
textured pattern using 12mm (US 17) needles.

Special abbreviations

cn = cable needle; **C6B** = slip next 3 sts onto
cn and leave at back of work, K3, then K3 from
cn; **C6F** = slip next 3 sts onto cn and leave at
front of work, K3, then K3 from cn.

BACK and FRONT (both alike)

Cast on 43 (45: 47: 49: 51: 53) sts using
12mm (US 17) needles.
Row 1 (RS): P1, *K1 tbl, P1, rep from * to end.
Row 2: Knit.
These 2 rows form textured patt.
Cont straight until work measures 42 cm,
ending with a WS row.
Shape raglan armholes
Keeping patt correct, cast off 3 sts at beg
of next 2 rows. 37 (39: 41: 43: 45: 47) sts.
Next row (RS): P2, patt to last 2 sts, P2.
Next row: Knit.
Next row (dec) (RS): P1, P2tog, patt to last
3 sts, P2tog tbl, P1.
Next row: Knit.
Rep last 4 rows 4 (4: 4: 4: 4: 3) times more.
27 (29: 31: 33: 35: 39) sts.
Next row (dec) (RS): P1, P2tog, patt to last
3 sts, P2tog tbl, P1.
Next row: Knit.
Rep last 2 rows 5 (5: 6: 6: 7: 9) times more,
ending with a WS row.
Cast off rem 15 (17: 17: 19: 19: 19) sts.

SLEEVES (both alike)
Cuff (knitted sideways)
Cast on 21 sts using 10mm (US 15) needles.
Row 1 (RS): K10, P1, K10.
Row 2: K4, P6, K1, P6, K4.
Rows 3 and 4: As rows 1 and 2.
Row 5: K4, C6B, P1, C6F, K4.
Row 6: As row 2.
Rows 7 and 8: As rows 1 and 2.
These 8 rows form cable patt.
Cont in cable patt for a further 48 (48: 48:
56: 56: 56) rows, ending with a WS row.
Cast off but do NOT break yarn.
Main section
With RS facing and using 12mm (US 17)
needles, pick up and knit 31 (31: 31: 35:
35: 35) sts evenly along one row-end edge
of cuff.
Beg with patt row 2, cont in textured patt as
given for back and front, inc 1 st at each end
of 2nd and 1 (1: 1: 2: 2: 2) foll 6th rows, then

on 2 (2: 2: 1: 1: 1) foll 4th rows, then on foll
alt row. 41 (41: 41: 45: 45: 45) sts.
Work 1 row, ending with a WS row.
Shape raglan
Keeping patt correct, cast off 3 sts at beg of
next 2 rows. 35 (35: 35: 39: 39: 39) sts.
Working all raglan decreases in same way as
back and front raglan armhole decreases, dec
1 st at each end of 3rd and 2 (2: 3: 2: 3: 3)
foll 4th rows, then on foll 10 (10: 9: 11: 10:
10) alt rows. 9 (9: 9: 11: 11: 11) sts.
Work 1 row, ending with a WS row.
Cast off.

MAKING UP

Press all pieces using a warm iron over a
damp cloth.
Join all 4 raglan seams using back stitch or
mattress stitch if preferred.

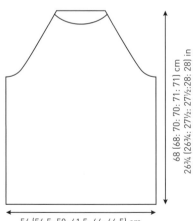

54 (56.5: 59: 61.5: 64: 66.5) cm
21¼ (22: 23: 24: 25: 26¼) in

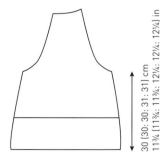

Continued on next page...

FAY

Recommendation

Suitable for the knitter with a little experience
Please see pages 40-42 for photographs.

	XS	S	M	L	XL	XXL	
To fit	**81**	**86**	**91**	**97**	**102**	**107**	cm
bust	32	34	36	38	40	42	in

Rowan Cashsoft 4 ply

| | 7 | 8 | 8 | 9 | 9 | 10 | x 50gm |

Photographed in Cherish

Needles

1 pair 2¼mm (no 13) (US 1) needles
1 pair 3mm (no 11) (US 2/3) needles
2.50mm (US C2) crochet hook

Buttons – 10

Tension

27 sts and 38 rows to 10 cm measured over
stocking stitch using 3mm (US 2/3) needles.

Special abbreviations

Tw2L = Knit into back of 2nd stitch, then knit
into front of first stitch.
MP = Make picot: cast on 1 st, cast off 1 st.
(See information page for details)

BACK

Lower back edging

Cast on 22 (22: 24: 24: 26: 26) sts using
2¼mm (US 1) needles and work as folls:
Row 1 (RS): MP, P to end.
Row 2: Knit.
Row 3: MP, K to end.
Row 4: P1, *P2tog, yrn, rep from * to
last st, P1.
Row 5: MP, P to end.
Row 6: Knit.
Row 7: MP, K to end.
Row 8: Purl.
Rep last 8 rows a further 21 (22: 23: 24: 25:
26) times more, then rows 1 – 6 again, ending
with a WS row.
Cast off, but do not break yarn.

Upper back

With RS facing and using 3mm (US 2/3)
needles, pick up and knit 118 (126: 134:
142: 150: 158) sts along straight edge
of lower back edging and cont as folls:
Next row (foundation row) (WS): K0 (2: 6:
0: 2: 6), P0 (2: 2: 0: 2: 2), *K10, P2, rep
from * to last 10 (2: 6: 10: 2: 6) sts,
K10 (2: 6: 10: 2: 6).
This row sets the sts for patt.
Cont in patt from chart, rep the 20 row patt
rep throughout, **and at same time** work
shaping as folls:
Work 4 rows, ending with a WS row.
Dec 1 st at each end of next and 3 foll 6th
rows.
110 (118: 126: 134: 142: 150) sts.
Work 5 rows, ending with a WS row.

Next row (dec) (RS): Work 2 tog, patt 2 (6:
10: 2: 6: 10), (P2tog, Tw2L, P2tog tbl, patt 6)
4 (4: 4: 5: 5: 5) times, patt 12, (P2tog, Tw2L,
P2tog tbl, patt 6) 3 (3: 3: 4: 4: 4) times, P2tog,
Tw2L, P2tog tbl, patt 2 (6: 10: 2: 6: 10), work
2 tog tbl.
92 (100: 108: 112: 120: 128) sts.
Work 23 rows in patt as set, ending with
a WS row.
Next row (inc) (RS): Inc in first st, patt 3 (7:
11: 3: 7: 11), (M1P, Tw2L, M1P, patt 8) 4 (4:
4: 5: 5: 5) times, patt 12, (M1P, Tw2L, M1P,
patt 8) 3 (3: 3: 4: 4: 4) times, M1P, Tw2L,
M1P, patt 3 (7: 11: 3: 7: 11), inc in last st.
110 (118: 126: 134: 142: 150) sts.
Cont in patt from chart, work 11 rows, ending
with a WS row.
Inc 1 st at each end of next and 3 foll
10th rows.
118 (126: 134: 142: 150: 158) sts.
Cont straight until back measures 29 (29: 30:
30: 31: 31) cm from pick-up row, ending with
a WS row.

Shape armholes

Keeping patt correct, cast off 5 (6: 6: 7: 7: 8)
sts at beg of next 2 rows.
108 (114: 122: 128: 136: 142) sts. **
Dec 1 st at each end of next 5 (5: 7: 7: 9: 9)
rows, then on foll 2 (3: 3: 4: 4: 5) alt rows,
and then on 4 foll 4th rows.
86 (90: 94: 98: 102: 106) sts.
Cont straight until armhole measures
18 (19: 19: 20: 20: 21) cm, ending with
a WS row.

Continued on next page...

Ronnie – Continued from previous page...

Collar (knitted sideways)

Cast on 33 sts using 10mm (US 15) needles.
Row 1 (RS): K22, P1, K10.
Row 2: K4, P6, K1, P6, K16.
Rows 3 and 4: As rows 1 and 2.
Row 5: K16, C6B, P1, C6F, K4.
Row 6: As row 2.

Rows 7 and 8: As rows 1 and 2.
These 8 rows form cable patt.
Cont in cable patt until one row-end edge
of collar, unstretched, fits neatly around entire
neck edge, ending after patt row 8 and with
a WS row.
Cast off.

Join cast-on and cast-off ends of collar then,
placing collar seam at centre back neck, sew
collar to neck edge, attaching collar so that
the "K4" section is left free.
Join side and sleeve seams.
Fold 4 sts to inside around lower edge of
sleeve and neatly slip stitch in place.

Shape shoulders and back neck

Cast off 6 (6: 7: 7: 8: 8) sts at beg of next 2 rows. 74 (78: 80: 84: 86: 90) sts.

Next row (RS): Cast off 6 (6: 7: 7: 8: 8) sts, patt until there are 10 (11: 11: 12: 12: 13) sts on right needle and turn, leaving rem sts on a holder.

Work each side of neck separately.

Cast off 4 sts at beg of next row.

Cast off rem 6 (7: 7: 8: 8: 9) sts.

With RS facing, rejoin yarn to sts on holder, cast off centre 42 (44: 44: 46: 46: 48) sts, patt to end.

Complete to match first side, reversing shapings.

FRONT

Work as given for back to **.

Dec 1 st at each end of next 2 rows.

104 (110: 118: 124: 132: 138) sts.

Shape neck

Next row (RS): Work 2 tog, patt 36 (38: 42: 44: 48: 50) and turn, leaving rem sts on a holder.

Work each side of neck separately.

Keeping patt correct, cast off 3 sts at beg and dec 1 st at end of next row.

33 (35: 39: 41: 45: 47) sts.

Dec 1 st at neck edge of next 5 rows, then on foll 2 alt rows, then on 3 foll 4th rows, then on foll 6th row **and at the same time** dec 1 st at armhole edge of next 1 (1: 3: 3: 5: 5) rows, then on foll 2 (3: 3: 4: 4: 5) alt rows, then on 4 (4: 4: 4: 3: 3) foll 4th rows.

15 (16: 18: 19: 22: 23) sts.

XL and XXL sizes only

Dec 1 st at armhole edge of (2nd: 4th) row, (21: 22) sts.

All sizes

Work 11 (11: 11: 11: 9: 7) rows, ending with a WS row.

Inc 1 st at neck edge of next and 2 foll 8th (8th: 8th: 10th: 10th 10th) rows.

18 (19: 21: 22: 24: 25) sts.

Cont straight until front matches back to start of shoulder shaping, ending with a WS row.

Shape shoulder

Cast off 6 (6: 7: 7: 8: 8) sts at beg of next and foll alt row.

Work 1 row.

Cast off rem 6 (7: 7: 8: 8: 9) sts.

With RS facing, rejoin yarn to sts on holder, cast off centre 28 (30: 30: 32: 32: 34) sts, patt to last 2 sts, work 2 tog.

Complete to match first side reversing shapings.

SLEEVES (work both the same)

Cuff edging

Cast on 18 (18: 18: 20: 20: 20) sts using 2¼mm (US 1) needles and shape side edge as folls:

Row 1 (RS): Purl.

Row 2: K3, wrap next st and turn.

Row 3: Purl.

Row 4: K10, wrap next st and turn.

Row 5: Purl.

Row 6: Knit.

Cont in patt as folls:

Row 7 (RS): MP, K to end.

Row 8: P1, *P2tog, yrn, rep from * to last st, P1.

Row 9: MP, P to end.

Row 10: Knit.

Row 11: MP, K to end.

Row 12: Purl.

Row 13: MP, P to end.

Row 14: Knit.

Rep rows 7 – 14 a further 11 (11: 11: 12: 12: 12) times, then rows 7 – 9 again, end with a RS row.

Next row (WS): K10, wrap next st and turn.

Next row: Purl.

Next row: K3, wrap next st and turn.

Next row: Purl.

Next row: Knit.

Cast off, but do not break yarn.

Main section

With RS facing and using 3mm (US 2/3) needles, pick up and knit 64 (66: 68: 70: 72: 74) sts along straight edge of cuff edging and cont as folls:

Next row (foundation row) (WS): K7 (8: 9: 10: 0: 0), P2 (2: 2: 2: 1: 2), *K10, P2, rep from * to last 7 (8: 9: 10: 11: 12) sts, K7 (8: 9: 10: 10: 10), P0 (0: 0: 0: 1: 2).

This row sets the sts for patt.

Cont in patt from chart, rep the 20 row patt rep throughout, **and at same time** work shaping as folls:

Inc 1 st at each end of 7th and every foll 8th (6th: 6th: 6th: 6th: 6th) row to 78 (80: 72: 92: 82: 108) sts then on every foll 10th (8th: 8th: 8th: 8th: -) row until there are 84 (92: 92: 100: 100: -) sts, taking inc sts into patt.

Cont straight until sleeve measures 26 (27: 28: 29: 30: 31) cm from pick-up row, ending with a WS row.

Shape top

Keeping patt correct, cast off 5 (6: 6: 7: 7: 8) sts at beg of next 2 rows.

74 (80: 80: 86: 86: 92) sts.

Dec 1 st at each end of next 3 (5: 5: 7: 7: 9) rows, then on foll 1 (2: 2: 3: 3: 4) alt rows, then on every foll 4th row until 54 sts rem.

Work 1 row, ending with a WS row.

Dec 1 st at each end of next and foll 4 alt rows, then on foll 3 rows, ending with a WS row.

38 sts.

Cast off 3 sts at beg of next 4 rows.

Cast off rem 26 sts.

MAKING UP

Press as described on the information page.

Join both shoulder seams using backstitch, or mattress stitch if preferred.

Neck edging

Cast on 8 sts using 2 ¼ mm (US 1) needles and work as folls:

Row 1 (RS): MP, P to end.

Row 2: Knit.

Row 3: MP, K to end.

Row 4: P1, *P2tog, yrn, rep from * to last st, P1.

Row 5: MP, P to end.

Row 6: Knit.

Row 7: MP, K to end.

Row 8: Purl.

Rep last 8 rows until straight edge of edging, when slightly stretched, fits around entire neck edge, starting and ending at left should seam and ending with patt row 8.

Cast off.

Join cast-on and cast-off ends of edging.

Pin out the edging onto a flat surface, stretching out the straight edge to form a curve and leaving the picot edge completely unstretched. Lightly steam, making sure the iron does not touch the knitting. Cover with a damp cloth and leave to dry naturally before unpinning. Slip stitch edging neatly in place around neck edge.

Sew sleeves into armholes. Sew side and sleeve seams, leaving side seams open along cast-on and cast-off edges of lower edgings. Using 2.50mm (US C2) crochet hook, make 5 button loops along each end of front edging and attach buttons to back edging to correspond.

54 [55: 56: 57: 58: 59] cm
(21¼ [22¾: 22: 22½: 22¾: 23¼] in)

40.5 (42.5: 45.5: 48.5: 50.5: 53.5) cm
(16 (16¾: 18: 19: 20: 21) in)

32 [33: 34: 35: 36: 37] cm
(12½ [13: 13½: 13¾: 14¼: 14½] in)

BACK, FRONT & SLEEVE

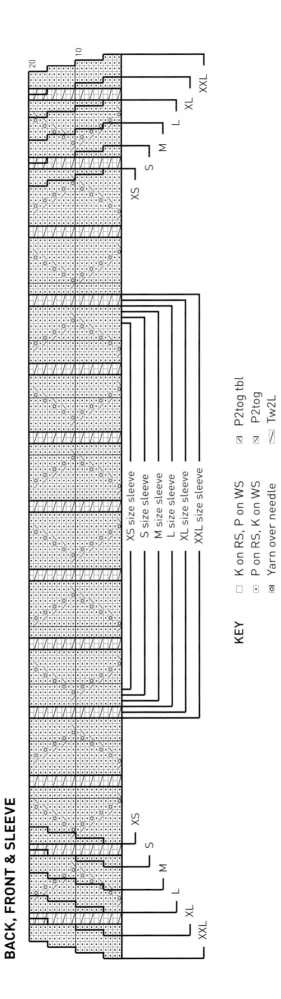

XS size sleeve
S size sleeve
M size sleeve
L size sleeve
XL size sleeve
XXL size sleeve

KEY

☐ K on RS, P on WS
· P on RS, K on WS
ᐤ Yarn over needle

☑ P2tog tbl
⊡ P2tog
⟋ Tw2L

Recommendation

Suitable for the knitter with a little experience
Please see pages 48 & 49 for photographs.

	XS	S	M	L	XL	XXL	
To fit	**81**	**86**	**91**	**97**	**102**	**109**	**cm**
bust	32	34	36	38	40	43	**in**

Rowan Kidsilk Haze

	5	6	6	6	7	7	x 25gm

Photographed in Anthracite

Needles

1 pair 2¾mm (no 12) (US 2) needles
1 pair 3mm (no 11) (US 2/3) needles
1 pair 3¼mm (no 10) (US 3) needles

Buttons – 9

Tension

25 sts and 34 rows to 10 cm measured over
stocking stitch using 3¼mm (US 3) needles.

EFFIE
BUTTON THROUGH SWEATER WITH FRILL TRIMS

BACK
Lower border
Cast on 20 (20: 23: 23: 25: 25) sts using
2¾mm (US 2) needles.
Row 1 (RS): Cast on 1 st, cast off 1 st, K to end.
Row 2: Purl.
Rows 3 and 4: Knit.
Row 5: Cast on 1 st, cast off 1 st, P to end.
Rows 6 and 7: Knit.
Row 8: Purl.
Row 9: Cast on 1 st, cast off 1 st, K to end.
Row 10: Knit.
Row 11: Purl.
Row 12: Knit.
These 12 rows form border patt.
Work the 12 border patt rows 16 (17: 18: 20:
21: 23) times more, then the first 8 (8: 8: 2: 2:
2) rows again, ending with a WS row.
Cast off but do NOT fasten off.
Main section
With RS facing and using 3¼mm (US 3)
needles, pick up and knit 95 (101: 107:
115: 121: 131) sts evenly along straight
row-end edge of lower border.
Beg with a **purl** row, cont in st st as folls:
Work 7 rows, ending with a WS row.
Next row (dec) (RS): K2, K2tog, K to last 4 sts,
K2tog tbl, K2.
93 (99: 105: 113: 119: 129) sts.
Working all decreases as set by last row,
dec 1 st at each end of 6th and 4 foll
6th rows.
83 (89: 95: 103: 109: 119) sts.**
Work 15 rows, ending with a WS row.
Next row (inc) (RS): K2, M1, K to last 2 sts,
M1, K2.
85 (91: 97: 105: 111: 121) sts.
Working all increases as set by last row, inc
1 st at each end of 6th and 2 foll 6th rows,
then on 5 foll 8th rows.
101 (107: 113: 121: 127: 137) sts.
Work 7 rows, ending with a WS row.
Shape armholes
Cast off 4 (5: 5: 6: 6: 7) sts at beg of next
2 rows.
93 (97: 103: 109: 115: 123) sts.

Dec 1 st at each end of next 3 (3: 5: 5: 7: 9)
rows, then on foll 3 (4: 4: 5: 5: 6) alt rows,
then on foll 4th row.
79 (81: 83: 87: 89: 91) sts.
Work 43 (45: 45: 47: 49: 47) rows, ending
with a WS row. (Armhole should measure
17 (18: 19: 20: 21: 22) cm.)
Shape shoulders and back neck
Cast off 7 (7: 8: 8: 8: 8) sts at beg of next 2 rows.
65 (67: 67: 71: 73: 75) sts.
Next row (RS): Cast off 7 (7: 8: 8: 8: 8) sts, K
until there are 12 (12: 11: 12: 12: 12) sts on
right needle and turn, leaving rem sts on
a holder.
Work each side of neck separately.
Cast off 4 sts at beg of next row.
Cast off rem 8 (8: 7: 8: 8: 8) sts.
With RS facing, rejoin yarn to rem sts, cast off
centre 27 (29: 29: 31: 33: 35) sts, K to end.
Complete to match first side, reversing shapings.

FRONT
Work as given for back to **.
Work 1 (5: 7: 9: 13: 13) rows, end with a WS row.
Divide for front opening
Beg and ending rows as indicated, working
chart rows 1 to 24 **once only** and then repeating chart rows 25 to 30 **throughout**, now place
chart as folls:
Next row (RS): K38 (41: 44: 48: 51: 56) and
slip these sts onto a holder for left front, work
next 28 sts as row 1 of chart, K to end. 45 (48:
51: 55: 58: 63) sts.
Work each side of front separately.
Next row: P17 (20: 23: 27: 30: 35), work last
28 sts as row 2 of chart.
These 2 rows set the sts – front opening edge 28
sts worked from chart with all other sts in st st.
Making buttonholes on chart rows 11 and 23
and then on every foll 12th row, cont as folls:
Work 12 (8: 6: 4: 0: 0) rows, ending with
a WS row.
Working all increases as set by back, inc 1 st at
end of next and 3 foll 6th rows, then on 5 foll
8th rows. 54 (57: 60: 64: 67: 72) sts.
Work 7 rows, ending with a WS row.

Shape armhole

Keeping patt correct, work 1 row, then cast off 4 (5: 5: 6: 6: 7) sts at beg of foll row.
50 (52: 55: 58: 61: 65) sts.
Dec 1 st at armhole edge of next 3 (3: 5: 5: 7: 9) rows, then on foll 3 (4: 4: 5: 5: 6) alt rows, then on foll 4th row.
43 (44: 45: 47: 48: 49) sts.
Work 19 (21: 21: 21: 23: 19) rows, ending with a WS row.

Shape neck

Next row (RS): Patt 11 (12: 12: 12: 13: 13) sts and slip these sts onto a holder, patt to end.
32 (32: 33: 35: 35: 36) sts.
Keeping patt correct, dec 1 st at neck edge of next 6 rows, then on foll 2 (2: 2: 3: 3: 4) alt rows, then on 2 foll 4th rows.
22 (22: 23: 24: 24: 24) sts.
Work 6 rows, ending with a **RS** row.

Shape shoulder

Cast off 7 (7: 8: 8: 8: 8) sts at beg of next and foll alt row.
Work 1 row.
Cast off rem 8 (8: 7: 8: 8: 8) sts.
With **WS** facing, rejoin yarn to rem sts, cast on 7 sts, then patt across these 7 sts and next 21 sts as row 2 of chart (beg and ending rows as indicated), P to end. 45 (48: 51: 55: 58: 63) sts.

Next row (RS): (K2, M1) 0 (0: 0: 0: 1: 1) times, K17 (20: 23: 27: 28: 33), work last 28 sts as row 3 of chart.
Complete to match first side, reversing shapings, omitting buttonholes and working first row of neck shaping as folls:
Next row (RS): Patt 32 (32: 33: 35: 35: 36) sts and turn, leaving rem 11 (12: 12: 12: 13: 13) sts on a holder.

SLEEVES (both alike)

Cast on 188 (196: 196: 204: 220: 228) sts using 3mm (US 2/3) needles and yarn **DOUBLE**.
Break off one strand of yarn and cont using yarn **SINGLE** as folls:
Row 1 (RS): *sl 1, K1, psso, rep from * to end.
94 (98: 98: 102: 110: 114) sts.
Row 2: Purl.
Row 3: As row 1.
47 (49: 49: 51: 55: 57) sts.
Beg with a P row, work in st st for 3 rows, ending with a WS row.
Place markers at both ends of last row.
Change to 3¼mm (US 3) needles.
Beg with a K row, work in st st for 20 rows, ending with a WS row.

Working all sleeve increases in same way as side seam increases, inc 1 st at each end of next and every foll 10th (10th: 10th: 8th: 10th: 10th) row to 65 (63: 75: 61: 75: 77) sts, then on every foll 12th (12th: -: 10th: 12th: 12th) row until there are 71 (73: -: 79: 81: 83) sts.
Cont straight until sleeve measures 45 (46: 46: 47: 48: 48) cm **from markers**, ending with a WS row.

Shape top

Cast off 4 (5: 5: 6: 6: 7) sts at beg of next 2 rows. 63 (63: 65: 67: 69: 69) sts.
Dec 1 st at each end of next 3 rows, then on foll alt row, then on foll 4th row, then on 2 (3: 3: 3: 4: 5) foll 6th rows. 49 (47: 49: 51: 51: 49) sts.
Work 3 rows.
Dec 1 st at each end of next and 0 (0: 1: 1: 0: 0) foll 4th rows, then on foll 4 (3: 3: 4: 5: 4) alt rows, then on foll 5 rows, ending with a WS row.
Cast off rem 29 sts.

40.5 (43: 45: 48.5: 51: 55) cm
16 (17: 18: 19: 20: 21½) in

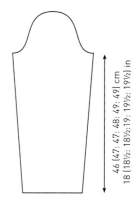

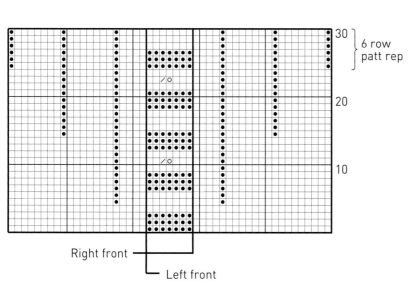

Right front
Left front

Key

☐ K on RS, P on WS

▣ P on RS, K on WS

⟋○ Right front only: yfwd, K2tog (to make a buttonhole)

Continued on next page...

EDIE

DEEP RAGLAN SWEATER WITH WIDE NECK

Recommendation

Suitable for the novice knitter
Please see pages 50 & 51 for photographs.

	XS	S	M	L	XL	XXL	
To fit	**81**	**86**	**91**	**97**	**102**	**109**	cm
bust	32	34	36	38	40	43	in

Rowan Kid Classic

	7	8	8	9	9	10x 50gm

Photographed in Smoke

Needles

1 pair 3¾mm (no 9) (US 5) needles
1 pair 4½mm (no 7) (US 7) needles

Tension

21 sts and 27 rows to 10 cm measured over
stocking stitch using 4½mm (US 7) needles.

BACK and FRONT (both alike)

Cast on 82 (88: 92: 98: 102: 112) sts using
3¾mm (US 5) needles.
Row 1 (RS): K0 (1: 0: 0: 0: 1), P0 (2: 1: 0: 2:
2), *K2, P2, rep from * to last 2 (1: 3: 2: 0: 1)
sts, K2 (1: 2: 2: 0: 1), P0 (0: 1: 0: 0: 0).
Row 2: P0 (1: 0: 0: 0: 1), K0 (2: 1: 0: 2: 2),
*P2, K2, rep from * to last 2 (1: 3: 2: 0: 1) sts,
P2 (1: 2: 2: 0: 1), K0 (0: 1: 0: 0: 0).
These 2 rows form rib.
Work in rib for a further 8 (8: 10: 10: 12: 12)
rows, ending with a WS row.
Dec 1 st at each end of next and 4 foll 8th
rows. 72 (78: 82: 88: 92: 102) sts.
Work 6 rows, ending with a **RS** row.
Next row (inc) (WS): Rib 4 (7: 1: 4: 6: 3), M1,
*rib 4 (4: 5: 5: 5: 6), M1, rep from * to last 4
(7: 1: 4: 6: 3) sts, rib 4 (7: 1: 4: 6: 3).
89 (95: 99: 105: 109: 119) sts.
Change to 4½mm (US 7) needles.
Beg with a K row, work in st st for 10 rows,
ending with a WS row.
Next row (inc) (RS): K3, M1, K to last 3 sts,
M1, K3. 91 (97: 101: 107: 111: 121) sts.
Working all increases as set by last row, inc
1 st at each end of 10th and foll 10th row,
then on 3 foll 6th rows.
101 (107: 111: 117: 121: 131) sts.
Work 5 rows, ending with a WS row.

Shape raglan armholes

Cast off 7 sts at beg of next 2 rows.
87 (93: 97: 103: 107: 117) sts.
Work 2 (2: 0: 0: 0: 0) rows.
Next row (dec) (RS): K1, K2tog, K to last 3 sts,
K2tog tbl, K1.
85 (91: 95: 101: 105: 115) sts.
Working all raglan armhole decreases as set
by last row, dec 1 st at each end of 6th (4th:
2nd: 2nd: 2nd: 2nd) and 2 (0: 2: 5: 8: 15)
foll 6th (0: alt: alt: alt: alt) rows, then on
9 (13: 13: 12: 11: 8) foll 4th rows.
61 (63: 63: 65: 65: 67) sts.
Work 3 rows, ending with a WS row.

Shape neck

Next row (RS): K1, K2tog, K10 and turn,
leaving rem sts on a holder. 12 sts.
Work each side of neck separately.
Dec 1 st at neck edge of next 7 rows **and at
same time** dec 1 st at raglan armhole edge
of 4th row.
4 sts.
Next row (RS): K1, K3tog.
2 sts.
Next row: P2tog and fasten off.
With RS facing, rejoin yarn to rem sts, cast
off centre 35 (37: 37: 39: 39: 41) sts, K to
last 3 sts, K2tog tbl, K1. 12 sts.
Complete to match first side, reversing shapings.

Effie - Continued from previous page...

MAKING UP

Pin the pieces out and steam gently without
allowing the iron to touch the yarn.
Join both shoulder seams using back stitch
or mattress stitch if preferred.

Neckband

With RS facing and using 2¾mm (US 2)
needles, slip 11 (12: 12: 12: 13: 13) sts from
right front holder onto right needle, rejoin yarn
and pick up and knit 28 (28: 28: 30: 30: 32)
sts up right side of neck, 35 (37: 37: 39: 41:
43) sts from back, and 28 (28: 28: 30: 30: 32)
sts down left side of neck, then patt 11 (12:
12: 12: 13: 13) sts from left front holder.
113 (117: 117: 123: 127: 133) sts.
Beg with a K row, work in rev st st for 3 rows,
ending a WS row. Cast off purlwise (on RS).

Frills (make 6)

Cast on 360 sts using 3mm (US 2/3) needles
and yarn **DOUBLE**.
Break off one strand of yarn and cont using
yarn **SINGLE** as folls:
Row 1 (RS): *sl 1, K1, psso, rep from * to end.
180 sts.
Row 2: Purl.
Row 3: As row 1. 90 sts.
Rows 4 and 5: Knit.
Cast off knitwise (on **WS**).
Neatly sew cast-off edge of each frill to each
vertical line of P sts up front, easing in fullness
if required.
Join side seams. Join sleeve seams. Insert
sleeves into armholes.
Neatly sew cast-on edge of left front in place
behind right front at base of front opening.
Sew on buttons.

SLEEVES (both alike)

Cast on 44 (44: 46: 48: 48: 50) sts using 3¾mm (US 5) needles.

Row 1 (RS): K0 (0: 0: 1: 1: 0), P1 (1: 2: 2: 2: 0), *K2, P2, rep from * to last 3 (3: 0: 1: 1: 2) sts, K2 (2: 0: 1: 1: 2), P1 (1: 0: 0: 0: 0).

Row 2: P0 (0: 0: 1: 1: 0), K1 (1: 2: 2: 2: 0), *P2, K2, rep from * to last 3 (3: 0: 1: 1: 2) sts, P2 (2: 0: 1: 1: 2), K1 (1: 0: 0: 0: 0).

These 2 rows form rib.

Work in rib for a further 6 (6: 8: 8: 10: 10) rows, ending with a WS row.

Inc 1 st at each end of next and foll 8th row. 48 (48: 50: 52: 52: 54) sts.

Work 6 rows, ending with a **RS** row.

Next row (inc) (WS): Rib 6 (4: 5: 6: 4: 5), M1, *rib 2, M1, rep from * to last 6 (4: 5: 6: 4: 5) sts, rib 6 (4: 5: 6: 4: 5).

67 (69: 71: 73: 75: 77) sts.

Change to 4½mm (US 7) needles.

Beg with a K row, work in st st for 4 rows, ending with a WS row.

Next row (inc) (RS): K3, M1, K to last 3 sts, M1, K3.

69 (71: 73: 75: 77: 79) sts.

Working all increases as set by last row, inc 1 st at each end of 4th and 10 (11: 12: 14: 15: 16) foll 4th rows, then on foll 10 (9: 8: 6: 5: 4) alt rows.

111 (113: 115: 117: 119: 121) sts.

Work 1 row, ending with a WS row.

Shape raglan

Cast off 7 sts at beg of next 2 rows. 97 (99: 101: 103: 105: 107) sts.

Work 0 (0: 0: 0: 2: 2) rows.

Working all raglan decreases in same way as for back and front raglan armhole decreases, dec 1 st at each end of next and every foll alt row until 27 (27: 29: 29: 31: 31) sts rem.

Work 1 row, ending with a WS row.

Cast off.

MAKING UP

Pin the pieces out pulling gently into shape and steam gently.

Join both front and right back raglan seams using back stitch or mattress stitch if preferred.

Neckband

With RS facing and using 3¾mm (US 5) needles, pick up and knit 26 (26: 28: 28: 30: 30) sts from top of left sleeve, 9 sts down left side of front neck, 35 (37: 37: 39: 39: 41) sts from front, 9 sts up right side of front neck, 26 (26: 28: 28: 30: 30) sts from top of right sleeve, 9 sts down right side of back neck, 35 (37: 37: 39: 39: 41) sts from back, then 9 sts up left side of back neck.

158 (162: 166: 170: 174: 178) sts.

Row 1 (WS): P2, *K2, P2, rep from * to end.

Row 2: K2, *P2, K2, rep from * to end.

These 2 rows form rib.

Cont in rib for a further 4 rows, ending with a **RS** row.

Cast off in rib (on **WS**).

Join left back raglan and neckband seam.

Join side and sleeve seams.

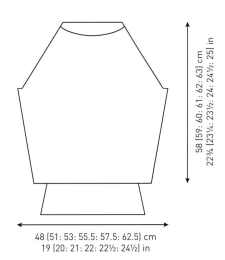

48 (51: 53: 55.5: 57.5: 62.5) cm
19 (20: 21: 22: 22½: 24½) in

58 (59: 60: 61: 62: 63) cm
22¾ (23¼: 23½: 24: 24½: 25) in

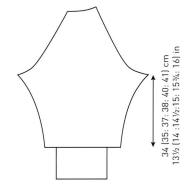

34 (35: 37: 38: 40: 41) cm
13½ (14 :14½:15: 15¾: 16) in

INFORMATION

TENSION

Achieving the correct tension has to be one of the most important elements in producing a beautiful, well fitting knitted garment. The tension controls the size and shape of your finished piece and any variation to either stitches or rows, however slight, will affect your work and change the fit completely.
To avoid any disappointment, we would always recommend that you knit a tension square in the yarn and stitch given in the pattern, working perhaps four or five more stitches and rows than those given in the tension note.

When counting the tension, place your knitting on a flat surface and mark out a 10cm square with pins. Count the stitches between the pins. If you have too many stitches to 10cm your knitting it too tight, try again using thicker needles, if you have too few stitches to 10cm your knitting is too loose, so try again using finer needles. Please note, if you are unable to achieve the correct stitches and rows required, the stitches are more crucial as many patterns are knitted to length.
Keep an eye on your tension during knitting, especially if you're going back to work which has been put to one side for any length of time.

SIZING

The instructions are given for the smallest size. Where they vary, work the figures in brackets for the larger sizes. One set of figures refers to all sizes. The size diagram with each pattern will help you decide which size to knit. The measurements given on the size diagram are the actual size your garment should be when completed. Measurements will vary from design to design because the necessary ease allowances have been made in each pattern to give your garment the correct fit, i.e. a

loose fitting garment will be several cm wider than a neat fitted one, a snug fitting garment may have no ease at all.

WRAP STITCH

A wrap stitch is used to eliminate the hole created when using the short row shaping method. Work to the position on the row indicated in the pattern, wrap the next st (by slipping next st onto right needle, taking yarn to opposite side of work between needles and then slipping same st back onto left needle – on foll rows, K tog the loop and the wrapped st) and turn, cont from pattern.

BEADING

Bead 1 (RS rows) = place a bead by bringing yarn to front (RS) of work and slipping bead up next to st just worked, slip next st purlwise from left needle to right needle and return yarn to back (WS) of work, leaving bead sitting in front of slipped st on RS. Do not place beads on edge sts of rows as this will interfere with seaming and picking up sts.

Beading note

Before starting to knit, thread beads onto yarn. To do this, thread a fine sewing needle (one which will easily pass through the beads) with sewing thread. Knot ends of thread and then pass end of yarn through this loop. Thread a bead onto sewing thread and then gently slide it along and onto knitting yarn. Continue in this way until required numbers of beads are on yarn.

WORKING A LACE PATTERN

When working a lace pattern it is important to remember that if you are unable to work a full repeat i.e. both the increase and corresponding decrease and vice versa, the stitches should be worked in stocking stitch or an alternative stitch suggested in the pattern.

CHART NOTE

Some of our patterns include a chart. Each square on a chart represent a stitch and each line of squares a row of knitting.

When working from a chart, unless otherwise stated, read odd rows (RS) from right to left and even rows (WS) from left to right. The key alongside each chart indicates how each stitch is worked.

FINISHING INSTRUCTIONS

It is the pressing and finishing which will transform your knitted pieces into a garment to be proud of.

Pressing

Darn in ends neatly along the selvage edge. Follow closely any special instructions given on the pattern or ball band and always take great care not to over press your work.

Block out your knitting on a pressing or ironing board, easing into shape, and unless otherwise states, press each piece using a warm iron over a damp cloth.

Tip: Attention should be given to ribs/edgings; if the garment is close fitting – steam the ribs gently so that the stitches fill out but stay elastic.
Alternatively if the garment is to hang straight then steam out to the correct shape.

Tip: Take special care to press the selvages, as this will make sewing up both easier and neater.

CONSTRUCTION
Stitching together

When stitching the pieces together, remember to match areas of pattern very carefully where they meet. Use a stitch such as back stitch or mattress stitch for all main knitting seams and join all ribs and neckband with mattress stitch, unless otherwise stated.

Take extra care when stitching the edgings and collars around the back neck of a garment. They control the width of the back neck, and if too wide the garment will be ill fitting and drop off the shoulder. Knit back neck edgings only to the length stated in the pattern, even stretching it slightly if for example, you are working in garter or horizontal rib stitch.

Stitch edgings/collars firmly into place using a back stitch seam, easing-in the back neck to fit the collar/edging rather than stretching the collar/edging to fit the back neck.

Straight cast-off sleeves: Place centre of cast-off edge of sleeve to shoulder seams. Sew top of sleeve to body, using markers as guidelines where applicable. Join side and sleeve seams.

Set-in sleeves: Join side and sleeve seams. Place centre of cast off edge of sleeve to shoulder seams. Set in sleeve, easing sleeve head into armhole.

CARE INSTRUCTIONS
Yarns
Follow the care instructions printed on each individual ball band. Where different yarns are used in the same garment, follow the care instructions for the more delicate one.

Buttons
We recommend that buttons are removed if your garment is to be machine washed.

ABBREVIATIONS

K	knit
P	purl
K1b	knit 1 through back loop
st(s)	stitch(es)
inc	increas(e)(ing)
dec	decreas(e)(ing)
st st	stocking stitch (1 row K, 1 row P)
garter st	garter stitch (K every row)
beg	begin(ning)
foll	following
rem	remain(ing)
rev st st	reverse stocking stitch (1 row P, 1 row K)
rep	repeat
alt	alternate
cont	continue
patt	pattern
tog	together
mm	millimetres
cm	centimetres
in(s)	inch(es)
RS	right side
WS	wrong side
sl 1	slip one stitch
psso	pass slipped stitch over
tbl	through back of loop
M1	make one stitch by picking up horizontal loop before next stitch and knitting into back of it
M1p	make one stitch by picking up horizontal loop before next stitch and purling into back of it
yfwd	yarn forward
yon	yarn over needle
yrn	yarn round needle
Mp	Make picot: Cast on 1 st, by inserting the right needle between the first and second stitch on left needle, take yarn round needle, bring loop through and place on left (one stitch cast on), cast off 1 st, by knitting first the loop and then the next stitch, pass the first stitch over the second (one stitch cast off).
Cn	cabl needle
C4B	Cable 4 back: Slip next 2 sts onto a cn and hold at back of work, K2, K2 from cn.
C4F	Cable 4 front: Slip next 2 sts onto a cn and hold at front of work, K2, K2 from cn.

THANK YOU!

Graham Watts, Diana Fisher, Kristie Stubley, Lee Davies,
Angela Lin, Sue Whiting, Tricia McKenzie, Ann Hinchcliffe,
Lindsay Hargreaves, Susan Laybourn, Ella Taylor, Arna Ronan,
Sandra Richardson, Mary Wilmot & Peter Fisher.

Our grateful thanks also go to,
Mr Denton & all at Holme Sunday school,
Mr & Mrs Howden & all at the Friends Meeting House, Wooldale,
and Helene & her girls at Revival Vintage – www.revivalvintage.co.uk

INDEX

GARMENT	PICTURE	PATTERN
AAREN	36 & 37	88
ARCHIE	26 & 27	80
AURA	28, 29 & 53	81
BEA	29	77
BILLIE	10 & 11	62
CHRISTY	35	85
DUSTY	30, 31 & 32	82
ED	39 & 41	92
EDIE	50 & 51	100
EFFIE	48 & 49	98
FAY	40 & 42	95
JEN	22 & 24	72
KAT	17, 36 & 52	91
LAUREN	20 & 21	69
LUCKY	38, 46 & 47	68
MAGGIE	19 & 34	66
NAT	23	74
RONNIE	6, 8 & 9	94
SID	12 & 13	64
THEA	15, 16 & 25	59
VIVIENNE	43 & 44	56
INFORMATION		102